Benjamin Britten and Montagu Slater's *Peter Grimes*

'Who can turn skies back and begin again?'

—Peter

This book contends that *Peter Grimes*, widely regarded as one of the greatest and most influential operas of the twentieth century, is also one of the British theatre's finest 'lost' plays. Seeking to liberate Britten and Slater's work from the blinkered traditions of theatre and opera criticism, Sam Kinchin-Smith poses two questions:

- If an opera was created like a play, and can be staged as a play, is it a play?
- If a portion of its success and influence is the product of this newly identified theatrical engine, is it then a great play?

The answers involve Wagner and W.G. Sebald, George Crabbe and Complicité, *Akenfield* and *Twin Peaks*.

Challenging long-established narratives of post-war theatre history, this book makes a compelling case for why practitioners and scholars of performance ought to pay more attention to Britten and Slater's achievement – a milestone of unconventional English modernism – and perhaps to other operatic masterpieces too.

Sam Kinchin-Smith, like Peter Grimes, was born in Suffolk and now lives on/in a boat. He works for the *London Review of Books* and has written for publications including the *New Statesman*, *Condé Nast Traveller* and the *Independent*.

The Fourth Wall

The Fourth Wall series is a growing collection of short books on famous plays. Its compact format perfectly suits the kind of fresh, engaging criticism that brings a play to life.

Each book in this series selects one play or musical as its subject and approaches it from an original angle, seeking to shed light on an old favourite or break new ground on a modern classic. These lively, digestible books are a must for anyone looking for new ideas on the major works of modern theatre.

www.routledge.com/performance/series/4THW

Also available in this series:

Coming soon:

Benjamin Britten and Montagu Slater's *Peter Grimes*

Sam Kinchin-Smith

Routledge
Taylor & Francis Group

LONDON AND NEW YORK

First published 2018
by Routledge
2 Park Square, Milton Park, Abingdon, Oxon OX14 4RN

and by Routledge
711 Third Avenue, New York, NY 10017

Routledge is an imprint of the Taylor & Francis Group, an informa business

© 2018 Sam Kinchin-Smith

British Library Cataloguing-in-Publication Data
A catalogue record for this book is available from the British Library

Library of Congress Cataloging-in-Publication Data
A catalog record for this title has been requested

ISBN: 978-1-138-67866-8 (pbk)
ISBN: 978-1-315-55881-3 (ebk)

Typeset in Bembo
by Out of House Publishing

For my parents, from whom I learned to love the music of the North Sea

Contents

List of figures

Acknowledgements

Thanks above all to Ben Piggott for asking me to write this book, and valuing its idiosyncrasies. It surely wouldn't exist if it wasn't for Talia Rodgers, who let me learn so much on the job, and Andrew O'Hagan, whose Suffolk shed and general vibes helped me feel like a writer. I'm grateful to everybody (especially Theo) who read bits; to Nico for always, somehow, finding the time to answer my dumb questions with super-human patience and generosity and eloquence; and to the Britten-Pears Foundation for the happy days I spent in their library and archive.

Back in 2013 Aldeburgh Music was kind enough to rustle up two press tickets for *Grimes on the Beach* the day before the last performance, but I never wrote the review I said I would, and have felt bad about it ever since. I hope this makes up for that, somewhat. Nancy agreed to drop everything and join me on my madcap dash to Suffolk and, as with all the formative art moments we have shared, her company is what I think of first when I remember that enchanted weekend, which is where this book began, and begins.

Grimes on the Beach

In June 2013, the Aldeburgh Festival celebrated its founder's centenary by staging his best-known opera in a manner that could hardly have done more to brutalise his music. *Grimes on the Beach*, a production of *Peter Grimes* that was performed over three nights on the very shoreline that first gave George Crabbe, and then Benjamin Britten, a setting for their stories of Suffolk fisherfolk life, submerged the composer's achievement in a site-specific storm of ambient sound. The orchestra was reduced to a recording, captured earlier in the week in the concert hall a few miles up the road at Snape Maltings, then squeezed through a hundred tiny speakers that distributed the sound efficiently, but with an emphasis dependent on the wind. The soloists were amplified, their voices disembodied, enunciating a few feet in front of each section of the audience, as their owners' mouths opened and closed fifty yards behind. The chorus maintained an increasingly heroic focus on Britten's matrix of time-signatures despite the drizzle in their eyes and the unrelenting beat and hiss of the tide. The combined effect was less a carefully proportioned seascape in the style of Paul Nash, more a Turner-ish splash.

A travesty, if we're to apply Britten's own standards of precision and interpretative priority.

But it was also a triumph: a revival charged with enough iconoclastic energy to force received notions into a somersault. I emerged from *Grimes on the Beach*'s internal life wide-eyed with the realisation that *Peter Grimes*'s external life – its place in the music and performance histories both of my own internal canon and, potentially, of everybody else's too – had been transformed: into something bigger, brighter, more universal.

In the manner of the earliest editions of Aldeburgh, which saw one-night-only theatrical productions programmed alongside recitals and concert performances (Brecht's *Good Person of Szechwan* in 1960, for example), the festival had staged a play. Aldeburgh Music had taken the work that re-established opera in English as a viable contemporary artform, and harried and flattened its orchestration into a single layer of the wider dramatic tableau. The music had brought colour and shade, momentum and eloquence, pattern, texture and metaphor to this *Peter Grimes*'s mise en scène, its choreography, its site-specificity, but none of these had felt defined or delineated by Britten's compositional intention. The work hadn't 'come out of' the music – *what opera does*, according to one theatre historian I spoke to early on in my research. A brilliantly original and potent performance event (Figure 1) had emerged instead from Britten's – and his librettist, Montagu Slater's – text's engagement with landscape and community, its exquisitely controlled narrative ambiguity, its latent theatrical dynamite.

To somebody like me, who knows a lot more about theatre than about opera, this made spellbinding sense. Britten's music had been liberated from a tightly wound musical

Figure 1 Still from the Prologue in the *Grimes on the Beach* film, directed by Margaret Williams (Grimes on the Beach Films Ltd, 2013).

algorithm, and offered a new life as a beautiful and original performance language. What was less explicable was that this was how the custodians of Britten's legacy had chosen to celebrate the centenary of a composer who, from his teenage years onwards, was synonymous with merciless musicological rigour and compositional seriousness. How could they have let this happen?

One pessimistic view, which found its way into a number of reviews,[1] implied that Pierre-Laurent Aimard, the Aldeburgh Festival's artistic director, was simply echoing the noughties mania for blockbuster site-specific events: that *Grimes on the Beach* was just another link in a chain with the National Theatre of Wales at one end and Secret Cinema at the other. That, in other words, once somebody had suggested staging

Peter Grimes on the very beach on which much of the opera's action takes place, on paper a vintage centenary idea, it was going to go ahead regardless of what this dramatic reinsertion of Britten into the East Suffolk landscape revealed about his work. Regardless of whether it wrecked the work, even.

It would be naïve to discount the part played by novelty in a production that began with what might have been the most expensive establishing shot in the history of opera. A spitfire flyby along the line of the horizon announced that this would be a 1940s *Grimes*, rather than one set in the first half of the nineteenth century, as Britten intended. But this is the least interesting angle from which to approach the logistical backstory behind *Grimes on the Beach*. Better, surely, to accept Aimard's suggestion[2] that this was community opera, as much as a site-specific one. Such sentiments sound like they're intended to be overheard by the Arts Council, but this one represents legitimate, joined-up engagement both with Britten, that pioneering creative producer, and with *Peter Grimes*. Britten's return to his native coastline and community, and the resulting festival charged with the gung-ho, provincial-meets-professional energy best encapsulated by the title of his work for children, *Let's Make an Opera!*, represent a lens through which much of his work should always be viewed. This applies most of all to *Grimes*, an opera about the insidious dynamics that inevitably unite a small-town community against an imaginative individual.

The temptation to see *Grimes on the Beach* as a community project, and to look for its origins and significance there, was heightened by its companion piece in the 2013 Aldeburgh Festival programme. *The Borough* was an intimate shard of immersive theatre created by Punchdrunk.[3] Taking *Grimes on the Beach*'s literalism even further, *The Borough* extracted

characters and storylines from Britten's opera and placed them
in settings all over Aldeburgh, from a fisherman's hut on the
beach, to a little cottage that played the part of Ellen Orford's
home, to the reedbeds on the edge of town. Audience mem-
bers explored each location alone, with the help of a head-
phone commentary and a small army of extras, including – in
the Britten tradition, and I mean that innocently – a number of small boys. The effect, experienced after *Grimes on the
Beach*, was that the town of Aldeburgh (at the best of times a
slightly unreal, too-perfect beach resort) became a huge stage
set. It was difficult to tell the difference between performers
and innocent tourists: is that woman in a vintage dress looking at me like that because she's in character, or is she looking
at me because I'm looking at her like I'm in character? It was
the ultimate fulfilment, arguably, of Britten's decision to create a festival in the town that gave him his first opera setting.

But when I saw *The Borough* the morning after *Grimes on
the Beach*, it wasn't community theatre I thought of so much
as just: *theatre*. By picking up characters and themes from
Britten's opera, and dropping them into a reasonably cutting-
edge work of contemporary performance, which relegated
Britten's composition to the status of incidental music,[4] *The
Borough* encouraged me to double-down on suspicions that
had already begun to crystallise. Perhaps the perversely original take on *Grimes* that I'd experienced the night before, in
which Britten's music represented a feature of the drama
rather than its origin, was in fact a justifiable response to the
emphases of Britten's performance text. A response rooted
in the revelation that the opera still worked, better than ever
actually, even as logistical challenges hammered away at the
music. Perhaps the director Tim Albery and the team behind
Grimes on the Beach had come to realise, whether consciously

or subconsciously, that Britten's achievement in his most famous opera is, primarily, theatrical rather than musical. And the right way to celebrate that was with two works of experimental theatre.

I left Suffolk increasingly confident that the impact of this performance event, perhaps the most significant of my life, was not so much the product of site-specific spectacle and community choreography as it was, quite simply, the work of Britten, Slater and the other artists there at the beginning, liberated from the opera house's proscenium. Albery staged a play because *Peter Grimes* is actually, literally, a play – by contemporary standards of what is and isn't theatre, anyway. Not in a way that means it isn't also music-theatre. But it might just be as good a play as it is an opera. And it's a great opera.

This is the case I will be making in this book, in order to justify its place in a series whose stated purpose is to interrogate 'modern theatre's best loved works'. That a Benjamin Britten who is illuminated by the bright lights of contemporary theatre, and the explosive transformations it has undergone in the last couple of decades in particular, deserves a place in theatre history that no critic has ever thought to give him. Because *Peter Grimes* is a performance text of such shattering originality and potency that, if it is staged in a way that gives its theatrical emphases the opportunity to face off against its music, it starts to look like a remarkable thing: a lost play, perhaps one of the twentieth century's finest.

For lost it has been, to the theatre-going world, even as it has been elevated to a unique status in the operatic canon: the centenary year alone saw three separate major revivals staged in the UK. With contemporary performance having arrived at a place where Katie Mitchell is more likely to be found directing an opera in Aix than a play in Avignon, it feels rather archaic to talk of different Worlds. But it is precisely the post-modern, post-genre performance theatre innovations of recent decades that highlight the one arena in which an apartheid persists: theatre history. Accounts of European and American theatre in the twentieth century either ignore opera totally, as in Routledge's gigantic *Theatre Histories: An Introduction*, in which 'opera' as a whole is afforded fewer than half the number of index references listed under 'Peter Brook', none of them referring to twentieth-century chapters; or they start to become interested from the moment when Philip Glass and Robert Wilson premiered *Einstein on the Beach* at Avignon rather than Aix, in 1976, and laid the groundwork for traditional distinctions to be subsumed within the unprecedentedly catholic category we now call avant-garde performance.

Most incomprehensible of all are narratives which recognise the post-genre future into which *Einstein* offered a portal, without then turning back and considering the 76 years of twentieth-century opera history that preceded it, wondering whether they too might represent part of the story of modern theatre. Historians and theatre critics are comfortable going back as far as Wagner, usually in order to erroneously deploy the word *Gesamtkunstwerk*, and might mention Berg's *Wozzeck* in a wider discussion of German Expressionism, but after that it's silence all the way through to the 1970s. To take one example, chosen because it's so blandly representative, Michael Billington's history of the twentieth-century British theatre, *State of the Nation*, doesn't once mention *Peter Grimes* and reduces Benjamin Britten to a single footnote. Not only that, but the reference relates to Ronald Duncan. He's a figure whose primary claim to fame in any multidisciplinary account of twentieth-century culture would be as one of Britain's greatest composer's most hapless librettist. But his part in Billington's story is as an underrated playwright who, 'having struck up a relationship with Benjamin Britten, who composed the incidental music for *This Way to the Tomb* … was invited to write the libretto for *The Rape of Lucretia*' (Billington, 27).

It's a bizarre situation, but one that's easily explained. Mostly it's the fault of theatre critics: for not leaving their comfort zones, and for not being more imaginative in applying the knowledge they have accrued to a greater range of artworks.[5] My theatre historian's assertion that most of the work of opera 'comes out of' the music reveals the likely roots of some of this reticence. Academics tend to pride themselves, in my experience, on what they know they don't know as much as on what they do. A sizeable section of theatre scholars probably don't know very much about music, on a theoretical level, so why should they apply themselves to a form of performance that originates in serious, difficult music?

Because critical engagement with music doesn't have to be conventionally theoretical, that's why. If the work represents pure, unmediated composition, then one can sympathise with academics hamstrung by their ignorance of musicological practice. But that's not what opera music is; the score only ever exists as part of a multidisciplinary artwork. And the moment music responds to, intersects with or catalyses something else, whether that be movement or acting or singing or lighting, that's the point at which anybody who knows anything about the other form has the right to stick their oar in. Because at that point music isn't just music anymore, it's dramatic art. That's why non-musicologists are justified in critiquing film music, or indeed incidental music in the theatre (Britten composed a good deal of both before he wrote

Grimes); why a critical vocabulary exists within both fields, rooted in film and performance theory[6] respectively rather than musicology. So why the lack of crossover opera criticism? Because the composition in opera is often the work of a genius, rather than a technician? Please: to claim one can't write critically about opera without a substantive grounding in musicological principles is akin to the discredited line of argument that one can't interrogate Shakespeare without an expert knowledge of early modern linguistics and philosophy. This notion has been shredded by the hands-on, iconoclastic work of practitioners of Shakespeare in performance, which has revealed practical realities central to the meaning of the plays that would never have been discovered through the enthusiastic mining of Erasmus and Petrarch. (This particular critical practice also reminds us that theatre-makers don't share theatre critics' reservations about engaging with opera: in the past couple of years I've seen operas directed by Phelim McDermott, Simon McBurney and Fiona Shaw, all of whom started out as theatre artists.)

And what about those operas like *Peter Grimes* which, I will be arguing, aren't anyway built out of their music? In such cases the critical closed-mindedness feels even more pronounced.

Opera-makers and critics also deserve a portion of the blame, however. Opera has consistently refused to absorb and respond to the discoveries of twentieth-century performance practice in a manner that would prove to people with serious thoughts about theatre that it's not just hysterical melodrama, that it's very much worth their time. This was particularly apparent in the case of one of the aforementioned centenary *Grimeses*: David Alden's production for the ENO, originally staged in 2009 and revived for the 2013/14 season. Looking forward to what I'd heard was a thrillingly experimental take on Britten, I found myself mostly nonplussed: why was everybody so excited about this pick-and-mix of early-twentieth-century pan-European avant-garde tropes, from Weimar Expressionism to Craigian übermarionettes, crow-barred into a production otherwise rooted in a realistic-ish depiction of 1940s Suffolk? And then I realised: opera audiences and critics hadn't seen most of this stuff on a stage before! Even though it's almost a century old! So it didn't matter that it was inelegantly deployed. A year or so earlier I'd seen Vakhtangov Theatre's take on *Uncle Vanya*, and the contrast between Alden's *Grimes* and that elegant integration of Meyerhold's techniques in the realisation of a classic text, so evidently the product of a century spent reconciling those two things, was stark.

As for the critics, I'll be looking in detail at the history of opera theorists thinking seriously about theatre in the next chapter, so for now I'll limit myself to a single illustrative reference. Reading the reflections of leading Britten scholar Donald Mitchell, on *Peter Grimes*, 50 years on, I was surprised to collide with the following passage:

> Perhaps the only comparable culture shock was to come a few years later, in 1956, but on that occasion in the theatre, when John Osborne's *Look Back in Anger* was first performed. There is not much in common between the opera and the stageplay, one may agree; but in one respect there is a fundamental shared feature: the protagonist of each drama, whether Peter Grimes or Jimmy Porter, is an anti-hero – wherein, though there were many other contributing factors in the case of the opera, resided each work's capacity to shock its audiences. Some may think

it a far-fetched suggestion, but I wonder in fact if, in a broad perspective, the opera did not play a part in the unshackling of a culture of which, later, Jimmy Porter was to be an icon?

(Mitchell in Banks, 125)

This one paragraph contains several of the received ideas I am hoping to counterbalance with this book. 'On that occasion in the theatre' – as though it's a different world. 'Though there were many other contributing factors in the case of the opera' – but not, I take it, in the play, an inferior, simplistic form. And, most strikingly of all, one seriously interesting and potentially important idea – that maybe the premiere of John Osborne's *Look Back in Anger* in 1956, a moment that for many critics represents modern British theatre's year zero, has origins which stretch back to an opera written a decade before. But expressed in the feeblest terms (they're both anti-heroes!) and never returned to in Mitchell's work. Why would he return to it, when there's the important business of a chord progression in Act 2 to attend to?[7]

In fact it's only the creators of music-theatre who escape blame. Which is not to ignore the fact that Britten was pretty conservative in his views about the correct way to stage an opera, particularly one of his own. But the texts themselves, and *Peter Grimes* in particular, suggest something else entirely.

It's tempting to interpret *Grimes on the Beach*'s title as a tacit acknowledgement of *Peter Grimes*'s right to be recognised as an intersection of the energies and imperatives of opera and performance every bit as significant as *Einstein on the Beach*. Alas, there's little evidence to suggest that Aldeburgh Festival's intention was anything other than to convert a coincidence into a neat joke. But this is the case I want to make, for both personal and canonical reasons.

To get My Journey out of the way first, *Grimes on the Beach* changed my life. I saw it at a time when I was increasingly bored by British theatre, which was failing to live up to the rich revelations of the performance theory I was steeping myself in at the time. The shapes, rhythms and politics of both Royal Court new writing and post-Complicité devised theatre were becoming, to my mind, complacent and self-serving, and I had started to seek solace in the cleansing novelty of performance art. My knowledge of orchestral music was shallow and reactive in a way that meant I was unlikely to look beyond 'cool' contemporary operas like George Benjamin's *Written on Skin* and Nico Muhly's *Two Boys* when buying tickets. Through Aldeburgh Festival's production of *Peter Grimes* I discovered that here, actually, was a text and a form that could represent everything I hadn't known I was looking for: a work pitched halfway between realism and expressionism, articulated through a performance language of exceptional complexity and beauty, driven by tireless community and ensemble energy, and straddling the line between English limitation – all folk culture, Anglicanism and the customs of my tribe – and the modernist avant-garde in a manner that felt like an honest expression of the dreary glories of British art.[8] That it was deeply rooted in the landscape in which I was born, a landscape which has also come to represent an important place both for my head and for my heart, meant the experience felt even more essential.

Lucky me. Although actually, that's precisely the point: I went to *Grimes on the Beach* on a whim, because it was an Event. I didn't go and see it for a reason that I've gone to see a lot of things in the past: the sense that certain cultural touchstones ought to be witnessed at least once, so that one 'has' them as a point of reference. I would have, but this wasn't a story I'd been told, which is illustrative. Because if *Peter Grimes* was a clichéd point of reference for anybody other than musicians and students of music, I think I would have known about it. I was editing books about theatre and performance at the time; my mother is a music teacher; but I just wasn't aware of *Grimes*'s importance. I'm not alone in this. One composer of music for theatre that I spoke to during my research told me that he 'didn't regard opera as relevant to my work. And then I saw *Peter Grimes*.'

In short, I have a personal stake in this. I think it's essential that *Grimes* is recognised as an unmissable gateway drug for audiences interested in all the possibilities of performance, to ensure that people like me don't miss out on it. But I want to go further still, and make the case that a reframed *Grimes* could also enrich theatre history itself. To return to the received ideas represented by Billington and Mitchell, my argument is that many of these are inverted by the recognition that *Peter Grimes* might be seen as a major theatre text. To be fair to Billington, *State of the Nation* challenges the notion that the 1940s and 1950s were a depressingly fallow period for the British theatre until John Osborne, *Waiting for Godot* and Joan Littlewood's Theatre Workshop came along. But how much stronger would his argument be if, alongside J.B. Priestley's efficient sermonising, Terence Rattigan's domestic claustrophobia and T.S. Eliot's desolate verse drama, he could deploy the most important and accessible opera in English for two centuries?

As for Osborne's and Littlewood's achievements, are they not complicated, somewhat, by the argument that the former's dramatic focus and the latter's call for 'a flexible theatre art, as swift-moving and plastic as the cinema, by applying the recent technical advances in light and sound and introducing music and the "dance theatre" style of production' (Goorney, 1981) were both foreshadowed, somewhat, by an opera that somehow sprang out of circumstances far less progressive than Osborne's Royal Court and Theatre Royal Stratford East, TW's home? An opera, that is, created by a composer 'greatly admired' by a figure whose work was a cornerstone of both Osborne's and Littlewood's practice, Bertolt Brecht.[9] Meanwhile, some of *Peter Grimes*'s most prominent themes, such as its pacifism, socialism and queer undertones, also have the potential to apply a compelling degree of pressure to established narratives of when and how British theatre was willing to reflect on such things.

The significance of a reframed *Grimes* that I find most potentially thrilling, though, is as a counterpoint to the post-*Einstein* narrative that suggests it was only when opera took on the abstract, minimalist, symbolist, postmodern qualities of Wilson and Glass that it became relevant to the contemporary practice of theatre. Accepting *Peter Grimes* as a play could open up Britten's toolbox – a set of unfashionable energies and English tropes as absent from contemporary performance as the phantoms of Wilson and Glass and the New York avant-garde remain over-represented – for a new generation of theatre-makers. Perhaps they'll create work that recaptures certain pre-postmodern qualities that have been lost, to the detriment of a post-postmodern moment which, not unconnectedly, seems to be finding so much value in other forms of anti-postmodern art, such as figurative painting and the New Sincerity movement in American poetry. Perhaps they'll then realise that interacting with Handel, too, and Wagner, or Berg, might mean uncovering more buried theatrical treasure, with very different but no less significant qualities.

But I'm getting ahead of myself. In order to argue that *Peter Grimes* can invert twentieth-century theatre history and enchant twenty-first-century theatre practice, I must first prove that it really is a play, and a great one at that.

Notes

1 For example, the *Guardian* on 18 June 2013 and the *New York Times* on 25 June 2013.
2 '*Grimes on the Beach* has encouraged us to take more risks … with a town, with the citizens there, with the community in the larger sense of the term – how to integrate everybody' (*Financial Times*, 23 May 2014).
3 The presence of Punchdrunk also played into the hands of those accusing the festival of site-specific spectacle, because of that company's misunderstood association with the Secret Cinema zeitgeist.
4 Incidental music, that is, which was also detached from its original context – so in Ellen's house, as she read a letter to herself, while I hid in a wardrobe and watched, it was Interlude V that started to play, through my headphones.
5 It wasn't always thus: Joseph Kerman's introduction to *Opera as Drama* lists the critics that 'musical drama has fascinated … almost as steadily as composers' – 'Saint Evremond, Addison, Diderot, Kierkegaard, Stendhal, Nietzsche, Shaw' (Kerman, 1).
6 A recent PhD summarises the theoretical framework outlined by Claudia Gorbman in film music theory's foundational text, *Unheard Melodies*: 'first, describing the shot sequence; second, considering shot length and its relative synchronicity with the score; third, conducting traditional but simplified musical analysis which establishes key, leitmotifs, melodic and thematic content and harmonic structure; and finally, applying her findings to an analysis of the music's function as it relates to the narrative' (Redner, 20).

7 Paul Kildea also makes the connection between *Grimes* and *Look Back in Anger*, and mentions Arthur Miller's *Death of a Salesman* (1949) too (Kildea, 248).

8 What Mitchell has called 'the paradox of *Grimes* … of its conspicuous turning of convention on its head while, at the same time, seeming to conform to convention, to sustain tradition' (Mitchell in Banks, 125).

9 Eric Crozier informed Britten, in a letter, that he'd come across 'a reference … to Brecht's great admiration for your music and the fact that he asked for some of your scores to be sent to him shortly before his death' (24 January 1959).

Opera as theatre

Peter Grimes is a play. It actually, literally, is a play: in one sense, this is an incontrovertible fact. *Grimes's* first director, Eric Crozier, describes the bizarre scenes by the merch stand at the American premiere in 1946:

> Slater, without our knowledge, avenged himself for the alterations that Ben and I had demanded over the previous two years and for the rewriting that Ben, Peter and I had found it necessary to do once the work was actually in rehearsal. He persuaded [Bodley Head] to bring out a volume that contained his original, unaltered, unperformed urtext. Copies of this version were on sale at the first night side by side with the libretto Ben had actually used.
>
> (cited in Banks, 49)

Slater's book was actually titled *Peter Grimes and Other Poems*, but the evidence that his libretto without music was swiftly picked up and used as a theatre script comes from a letter he sent Britten in November 1947: 'A young South African producer called ... to say could he please do P.G. as a play in Pretoria ... they can't have any music in this production unless on disk, but they're avid for any recordings they can get of the interludes' (30 November 1947).

This quirk of history represents both a wrong turn in, and an important detail of, my argument that *Peter Grimes* the opera is a work of both music-theatre and theatre-theatre. On the one hand, to suggest that it proves *Grimes* is a play would imply that any opera which has been published as a libretto without music is also a play, undermining *Grimes*'s special claim to theatrical status. On the other, the fact it was Slater himself, a playwright as well as a librettist, who went out of his way to publish a version of the text without music, does suggest that an important part of the case for *Peter Grimes* the play is to be found in the creation of Slater's libretto. As does the way he introduced his subversive little volume:

> In writing it I worked in the closest consultation with the composer, Benjamin Britten, from the moment when he first suggested the theme. We worked very much as a script-writer and director work on a film, the composer in this case being the director. The comparison has value, because for several reasons I believe it is useful at the present moment to dwell on how much there is in common between the arts of drama, opera, radio and film.
>
> (Slater, 7)

Before exploring the theatre-like ways in which *Grimes* came together prior to its first performances at Sadler's Wells in 1945, it's worth turning first to the wider history of people thinking about the theatre that exists within opera. Is there a critical tradition within which such a story can be understood, an agreed theoretical method for establishing proof?

It began with Wagner. The theoretical basis of the *Ring* cycle, which its author hoped would represent the ultimate synthesis of absolute music and dramatic seriousness, was a work called *Opera and Drama*, published for the first time in 1851. In characteristically intense prose, thick with metaphysical imagery and exclamation marks and grand aphorisms about Art and the Poet, the Artwork and the Public, Wagner called out the entire history of opera up to 'our present day' in the following terms:

> I declare aloud that *the error in the art-genre of Opera consists herein*: that a Means of expression (Music) has been made the end, while the End of expression (the Drama) has been made a means.
>
> (Wagner, xxxii)

The unhappy results of this error fail primarily on the level of text. For too long, 'the Poet [has taken] his inspiration from the Musician' and constructed 'his drama with a single eye to the specifically musical intentions of the Composer' resulting in operas 'to which "texts" thrown together into a semblance of dramatic cohesion were added waywardly as underlay'. Writers unwilling to accept that their sole purpose is to 'afford Music with a colourable pretext for her own *excursions*' will 'be content to be looked on as unserviceable for the post of opera-librettist' (Wagner, xxxiii–xxxiv).

But it's also a problem of synthesis. Wagner presents close readings of scenarios in which a lack of shared purpose and equality of authority between Poet and Musician results in absurdly self-contradicting work, such as when a

> gesture explained by the orchestra is of downright deci-
> sory importance ... The poet wishes, however, to deduce
> from this situation its 'necessary' successor, and this aim of
> his can only be realised by letting us feel that the mood
> is *not* completely satisfied ... He is concerned to make us
> recognise that the seeming quietude of his dramatis per-
> sonæ is merely a self-illusion ... [and inserts a gesture of]
> *foreboding*, while the orchestra is to elucidate the character
> of that foreboding ... But [what if, in performance] *this
> threatening gesture is omitted*; the situation leaves on us the
> impression of complete appeasement; merely the orches-
> tra, contrary to all expectation, suddenly strikes in with
> a musical phrase whose sense we have not been able to
> catch from the earlier utterances of a speechless singer ...
> (Wagner, 282–3)

Both problems will be solved by inverting the error, by '*erecting the genuine Drama on the basis of Absolute Music*' (Wagner, xxxiv). In order to achieve this the writer and the composer must be unshackled from the errors of the past, and encouraged to fulfil the respective potentials of their craft. For the writer, that's '*verse* [which is] the own-est poem of the Artist of the Present, begotten by his most peculiar fac-ulty, engendered by the fulness of his yearning' (Wagner, 289). If that sounds rather demanding, pity the composer, whose responsibility is to express the inexpressible and the trans-cendent, the true fabric of art: 'the water-mirror of the har-monic ocean of the Future ... the clear-seeing eye wherewith this Life gazes upwards from the depth of its sea-abyss to the radiant light of day' (Wagner, 289). Both strands of work must then be synthesised to the point that the joins are invisible and both halves of the artwork are united in their common goal – unmitigated Drama:

> the Orchestra is irresistibly to guide our whole attention *away from itself* as a *means of expression*, and direct it to the *subject expressed*. So that the very richest dialect of the Orchestra is to manifest itself with … *not being heard at all*: to wit, not heard in its *mechanical*, but only in its *organic* capacity, wherein it is One with the Drama.
>
> (Wagner, 284–5)

The influential opera theorist Joseph Kerman took up the baton almost exactly 100 years later with a book that positioned itself in a dialogue with Wagner from its title onwards: *Opera and Drama* became *Opera as Drama*. Motivated by similar frustrations to Wagner – with the unwillingness of critics and makers of opera to reflect seriously on the distinction between a supposedly 'dramatic' plot and truly dramatic art – Kerman also adopted two of Wagner's principal positions: that it's through an alchemical synthesis of text and music that opera becomes something greater than the sum of its parts, becomes Drama; but that it's ultimately music that's responsible for imbuing opera with its truly transcendental layers, its inexpressible truths. Where Kerman deviates from Wagner is in terms of what he wants to achieve with this theoretical blueprint. He's a critic, not an artist, so he's interested in applying it to opera history, rather than the creation of the Artworks of the Future. Indeed, he specifically wants to rescue Wagner's theory from its 'dialectical march to a *Gesamtkunstwerk*' (Kerman, 3) in order to prove that all pre-Wagnerian opera isn't in fact a write-off: it's the usual mixture of wheat and chaff that needs to be separated via an application of the principles of opera as drama, in order to drag contemporary opera culture out of a nosedive in which it can't tell the difference between the art of, say, Mozart and the 'kitsch' of Puccini.

Philip Brett, another musicologist, then applied Kerman's work to Britten for the first time, another half century or so later. He wanted to interrogate 'the many other people involved in the construction' of operas like *Peter Grimes*, and challenge the image of 'the reclusive magician of Aldeburgh, drawing to him those he needed to realise his ambitions' (Banks, 53–4), an important intervention I will return to.

I agree with much of Kerman's reinvention of Wagner's project, not least his characterisation of opera critics, which resembles my own:

> Most of them, I think, do not even recognise the problem. Perhaps they are to be excused for having an elementary notion of drama; but with *Tosca* as a dramatic idea, 'opera as drama' really has no import at all … dramatic unawareness underlies almost all current writing about opera, from the most philistine to the most professional.
>
> (Kerman, 11–12)

And his close-reading of the expansive interactions between libretto and composition in Good Opera, and the lack thereof in Bad Opera, represents an unsurpassed model for an assessment of some of the places where an opera like *Grimes* reveals itself to be great theatre, as well as great drama. We part ways because of that distinction, though. The main difference between Wagner's and Kerman's project and my own is that I am hoping to benefit the audiences, critics and makers of theatre by showing why they can and should accommodate certain operas in their canon. Their aim was to enrich a necessarily separate opera culture through the prioritisation of certain artworks and practices. Kerman and I define theatre very differently. My characterisation would have been unthinkable to the author of *Opera as Drama*, which was first published in 1952, the year before Joan Littlewood moved into Stratford East – and my attempt to move his conversation with Wagner on, from *Opera and Drama* to *Opera as Drama* to 'opera as theatre', the title of this chapter, would have been incomprehensible.

Which is not to say that Kerman didn't recognise that there was a dialogue between opera and theatre that could go both ways: 'musicians', he admitted, 'are no duller in the theater than literary men are in the concert hall' (Kerman, 11–12). But, for Kerman, theatre's apogee was verse drama of the kind created by Shakespeare and, more recently, T.S. Eliot, a form that – ironically – would essentially die out for a couple of generations shortly after *Opera as Drama* was published. On the basis of a comparison between this version of theatre and opera, he concluded that their purpose is fundamentally different: theatre's place is to be precise and intellectual, opera's to be direct and profound. My argument, charged with examples of plays that are willfully imprecise, direct and profound, is that great theatre can be both at the same time. Intriguingly, the seeds of such an expansive view of theatre do occasionally reveal themselves in *Opera as Drama*, for example in Kerman's recognition that 'music is also a natural medium for the projecting of various kinds of mood and pageantry, and is so used in the spoken theater' (Kerman, 9). But they're quickly shut down by his instinctive tendency to look towards the past, rather than the present (at one point he refers to 'Ibsen, Shaw and their less serious followers' [Kerman, 4]), and his suspicions about the innovations that would bring the two forms to the point of closeness they enjoy today. To Kerman, in 1952, 'a serious search for dramatic values' was being stifled by 'peripheral topics like opera in English, "modern" production methods, and television techniques' (Kerman, 3), rather than (as actually proved to be the case) furthered by them.

In short, there is an established critical tradition of identifying and reflecting on the powerful theatrical engine that exists within some operas, and doesn't within others, which can and should be channelled when assessing a work of music-theatre's claim to theatrical significance. But, because of a lack of interest in theatre on the part of those who have created it, and the limitations of their sense of what theatre is and can be, this discourse has been silent on the question of whether opera can be 'One with the Drama' to the point that it might cross over into the territory of theatre, and the consciousness of theatre people. That's what I find most irritating about Kerman's position, actually: the inference that theatre audiences aren't so interested in the direct and the profound.

Instead of listing all of the ways in which the post-Eliotic theatre expanded its own parameters, I want to outline some developments that help characterise the creation of *Peter Grimes* as a theatrical endeavour, as well as an operatic one. Two trends are particularly relevant: the first is the remixing of the traditionally top-down relationship between playwright, director and performers into something approaching collective ensemble responsibility (whether this begins when a company starts rehearsing a script, or at the very start of the creative process, as is sometimes the case with devising companies). The second, often related to this, is the shift towards a multimedia theatre, in which musicians have a central role in the creation of new work, on a level with the designer, say; and in which shapes, techniques and effects are borrowed from other art forms, such as cinema or dance.

Fully devised theatre of the kind produced by Complicité and Frantic Assembly, created by an ensemble of multidisciplinary artists given the space to explore a subject through trial and error in order to create a tapestry of vignettes, is often said to have originated in the process by which Theatre Workshop created *Oh, What a Lovely War!* (1963). I see it as a logical extrapolation of a theatre that more generally acknowledges that a script produced in isolation, then dictated by a director, isn't a blueprint for performance that makes full use of the collaborative and exploratory energies of an ensemble. Theatre critics have long recognised the implications this has for their practice, but opera criticism is still catching up. Brett still felt the need, in 1996, to explain that 'musical scholarship has been involved for a long time in exclusive notions of authorship and authority' which don't acknowledge 'the many other people involved in the construction of an opera – librettist, scenic and lighting designers, stage director, as well as singers, orchestra and conductor' (Brett in Banks, 55). This is ironic because one could argue that opera has been a fundamentally collaborative art for much longer than theatre because of its dependence on a composer, a librettist, a director, a conductor and a designer (though Wagner tried to be all of the above). The way in which a new opera comes together, according to the working practices of one composer I spoke to, anyway – with scenarios sketched, fleshed out and reordered, then given to a librettist who works them up into scenes, which are batted back and forth with the composer as he/she starts to assemble the melodic scaffolding, in the form of a short score for piano which, when complete, is put on its feet in rehearsal, where both music and text will be re-arranged again by the authors and director into something that pops, dramatically, at which point the process of full orchestration can begin, then and only then, 'because there's no time to change things once you have the band' – resembles ensemble theatre-making more than some traditional theatre practices do.[1]

Britten obscured the range and impact of the collaborative, editorial energies behind his work with composition sketches which enshrined 'all those values to which we have been held accountable: the composer's intention manifest in all its pristine glory; the musico-dramatic thought laid bare on the pencilled page, untrammelled by the exigencies of the opera house' (Banks, 55). But *Peter Grimes* was an intensely collaborative production, whose commonalities with the practice of ensemble theatre-making also served to increase the number of theatrical elements in the finished work. This began with its famous genesis, when Britten found a volume of George Crabbe's poetry in a bookshop in Los Angeles which, along with a *Listener* essay about the poet by E.M. Forster, uncorked in him a homesickness so profound he soon left the creative milieu he'd followed to America in 1939 and came home. 'The story of the beginning of the idea of the work is familiar enough', suggests Brett. 'Less familiar is the notion of how many people and connections were involved even at that moment' (Brett in Banks, 56). Christopher Isherwood, for example, was totally dismissive of 'the idea': 'I'm sorry, but I don't see any possibility of collaborating with you … on the

Peter Grimes libretto', he wrote to Britten. 'Frankly the subject doesn't excite me so much that I want to *make* time for it' (cited in Kildea, 185).

Britten's first major creative partner on the project was the man who had become his partner in life, Peter Pears, the tenor who would create the character of Peter in the first incarnation of *Grimes*, and many subsequent productions. He and Britten exchanged sketches (Figure 2) on the voyage back from America. Pears brought a practical theatrical brain to proceedings, no doubt rooted in his stage experience: in one early scenario he included a note that there should be 'just time for the landlord to emerge in front of his pub and have an aria'.[2] It was with the appointment of Slater, though, with whom Britten had worked in the past on documentary and theatre projects, that he found a creative foil from which real collaborative energy – and friction – would spark. Their partnership began promisingly: 'M has taken to *Grimes* like a duck to water & the opera is <u>leaping</u> ahead', Britten wrote to Elizabeth Mayer; 'I'm very keen on his whole attitude to the subject – very simple, full of respect for Crabbe, and with real stage experience' (4 May and 5 June 1942). Paul Kildea's biography of Britten identifies two 'key' episodes Slater introduced in the first phase of their collaboration, notable for their potent theatricality: 'the villagers' procession to Grimes's hut, hell-bent on confronting him over his behaviour, and the ecstatic, orgiastic manhunt in the third act' (Kildea, 219). Brett defines the librettist's contribution in more general terms: 'Slater appears to have been the one who saw how to improve the dramatic mechanics in order to turn the story from what might have been a horrifyingly senti-mentalized attempt to recuperate a child abuser into a taut localized social drama with universal implications about the

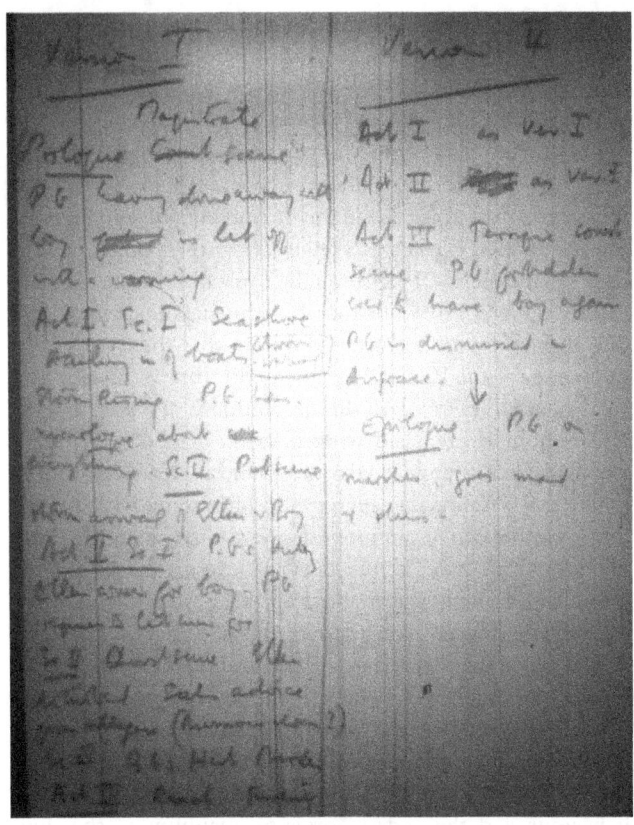

Figure 2 Two early attempts to organise *Peter Grimes* into acts and scenes, photographed at the Britten-Pears Archive.

precarious balance of responsibility between society and the individual' (Brett in Banks, 62).

Much of Slater's contribution to *Grimes*'s theatrical success was the product of the breakdown of his relationship with Britten, though, rather than its first, happy phase. Uniquely among Britten's librettists, Slater was willing to stand up to the composer in order to preserve essential components of *Grimes*'s dramatic shape. Kildea describes 'a whip-smart letter to Britten in December 1944, [in which Slater] fought to keep the women's quartet in Act 2 of *Grimes*, which at the time Britten was attempting to jettison' (Kildea, 265). One wonders how many more reviews would have taken the line of Hubert Foss in the *Listener*, who regarded Ellen as a 'pasteboard character', 'too good to be true or explainable' (Kildea, 235), if this gorgeous articulation of the female hinterland of the opera hadn't made Britten's final draft. This style of working relationship, culminating in the publication of Slater's 'poem', is one Britten did his best to avoid for the rest of his career, switching librettists almost as regularly as he switched subject matter.

Opinion is divided about which collaboration was the most effective. For Crozier it was *Billy Budd*, the work of E.M. Forster: 'Everyone who loves opera wants you & Morgan [Forster] to work together again', he wrote in a letter to Britten (8 December 1951).[3] Perhaps that's the point though: 'who loves opera'. Slater was best for theatre, a point proved by the libretto of the opera that came next, *The Rape of Lucretia*, on which Britten worked with a librettist much happier to roll over and have his tummy tickled, Ronald Duncan. Duncan's approach to creative tension is revealed by a letter in which he wrote to Britten that, 'as you must know, I am in entire agreement with everything you say' (3 June

1946). The result was an opera which made the critic Ernest Newman ask himself and his readers: 'what has become of Mr Britten's sense of the theatre and his feeling for his dramatic subject?' (cited in Kildea, 277). Most blameworthy are its overwrought dramatic tropes, one borrowed from an early draft of *Grimes*, and some really miserable poetry. *Lucretia* is framed by the observations of a double act of narrators, an idea Britten originally wanted to integrate into *Grimes*, in the form of 'a gendered [opposition] in which male and female choruses take separate roles, and disagree over Ellen's crucial dramatic gesture' (Brett in Banks, 55). And it's impossible to imagine Slater writing the line: 'the oatmeal slippers of sleep creep through the city and drag the sable shadows of night over the limbs of light' (Act 1, Scene 2).[4]

Duncan also worked on *Grimes*, rather more effectively, no doubt because he too was constrained here by collaboration. He describes his role rewriting the 'mad scene' of Act 3:

> [I] devoted myself to doing any cobbling to the libretto which Ben required. This wasn't easy since the words were, apart from the last scene, already set. It entailed finding lines to fit the precise run and stress of the music ... I sketched out the last scene, deliberately echoing phrases from arias and numbers in the earlier part of the opera so as to force Ben to take the opportunity of recalling phrases for the music.
>
> (cited by Philip Reed in Banks, 44)

As well as representing further evidence of how many people were involved in the making of *Grimes*, this account reveals how the traditional relationship between text, music and stage business was twisted and inverted by the opera's improvised genesis in the manner of trial-and-error ensemble theatre. Kildea describes how Britten's necessary 'problem solving, not strategic planning' resulted in new textures, 'an extension to an Interlude in *Peter Grimes*, say, [which] the staging required – which nudged the piece in a new, unexpected direction' (Kildea, 152). Duncan's work was just one facet of a wider process of revision taking place in rehearsal. 'Peter & I are pretty well re-writing his part', Britten told Duncan in a letter. 'Montagu agreed to the new mad-scene, and I kept your part in it fairly quiet, altho I murmured that you helped us a bit' (cited in Banks, 44). Britten would remember this dynamic editorial process when he was working on *Billy Budd* three years later: 'Erwin [Stein] tells me they're planning to engrave the vocal score right away', he wrote in a letter to Crozier. 'Is that wise? I may make hundreds of radical changes, right up to the 1st night' (19 February 1948).

Rehearsals were led by Crozier and Britten's two leads, Pears and the first Ellen, Joan Cross, to whom the director of Sadler's Wells, Tyrone Guthrie, wrote before the first night (reflecting her substantive role in *Grimes*'s creation): 'I absolutely support the policy of doing this opera; & congratulate you on the grit with which it has been carried thro' in the face of difficulties' (cited in Banks, 45). Crozier described his own part in the following terms: 'The truth is the characterisation of the opera imposes on the producer the responsibility of shaping his materials – singers, scenery, lighting – into a consistent whole, with a care for detail and a logic of emotion that are more often to be found in the production of drama than opera' (cited in Banks, 8). Judging from his production notes, it's clear that his priorities were clarity, coherence and practical matters of choreography, although there is evidence of another ensemble energy he contributed to the work, mostly unrecognised in the libretto and the score: 'The crowd is a vital element throughout the whole scene, although it sings only a small part of the time' (cited in Banks, 9), he notes with regard to the Prologue. It's also clear that he believed the opera contained the seeds of a theatrical expression he was unable to fully articulate this time round: 'I hope that other producers and designers, blessed with more adequate stages, will explore the value of a more poetic realism in its staging' (cited in Banks, 7).

Peter Grimes was an opera, then, that deviated extensively from its composer's intentions as a result of interventions by a number of powerful, opinionated figures. A number of Britten's subsequent career moves, from embracing chamber opera, to setting up a company and a festival, to changing librettist as regularly as he did, attest to his preference for a different kind of opera-making. But the collaboration of Britten, Slater, Pears, Duncan, Crozier, Cross and Kenneth Green, the designer, resulted in a work greater than the sum of its parts. Which is to some extent the definition of devised theatre.

Less distinct as a genre and practice, but no less important in the development of theatre over the past 70 years, has been its progress towards multimedia forms in which music and cinematic effects represent a major part of the dramatic tableau, without quite pulling it into the territory of music(al) theatre or immersive cinema. Complicité, again, offer the most prominent example of how far cinematic theatre has come, from the projections and cutaway transitions between scenes in *A Disappearing Number* (2007) to the *Bourne*-style GPS zooms that established locations in *The Master and Margarita* (2012), to artistic director Simon McBurney's *The Encounter*

(2015), which took the form of a binaural soundscape experienced, like *The Borough*, through a pair of headphones. And while music's role can be traced back to theatre's origins, I would argue it has never been so central in the creation and revival of plays as it is now. As many theatre companies as opera houses have commissioned work from Muhly, a leading contemporary composer, in recent years (although the former rarely ask for more than ten minutes of incidental music, so the comparison is of limited value). A 2015 production of *The Skriker* for the Manchester International Festival was billed, on its own website, as 'with Maxine Peake. By Caryl Churchill. Music by Nico Muhly and Antony.' The director's name didn't appear. Further evidence is provided by productions of three plays from the same era as *Peter Grimes* that I saw while researching this book: J.B. Priestley's *An Inspector Calls*, T.S. Eliot's *The Cocktail Party* and Terence Rattigan's *The Deep Blue Sea*. None of them has a script that calls for a soundscape, but all three productions relied on one of considerable prominence.[5]

The pioneers of this kind of theatre were the reference points I keep returning to: Littlewood's Theatre Workshop and, before that, the 'epic' theatre of Bertolt Brecht, which used music and projections and alienating effects to detach an audience from the drama playing out in front of them. It wouldn't be until after *Peter Grimes*'s premiere that Britten would (indirectly) work with Brecht.[6] But, in the years leading up to the war, Auden drew him into a loose collective of artists that made movies for the GPO Film Unit and plays for the Group Theatre and might be characterised as a halfway house between Brecht's Berliner Ensemble and the Theatre Workshop (TW). The way in which the Group Theatre (unrelated to the company of the same name started by Lee Strasberg in New York in 1931) defined its mission foreshadowed both Littlewood's manifesto and the ambitions of the English Opera Group that Britten would found after *Peter Grimes*. 'The Group Theatre was a vital part of Britten's apprenticeship', Kildea writes. 'The concept, which they drafted in an early statement, was simple yet unusual for the time: "by continually playing together and using its own producers, playwrights, painters, musicians, technicians, etc., to produce a company, which will work like a well-trained orchestra"' (Kildea, 114).

Britten worked on film and theatre projects throughout the 1930s; indeed, as Kildea puts it, 'there was considerable overlap in his music for film, theatre, radio and concert hall' (Kildea, 109). He created title and incidental music for GPO films including *Coal Face* (1935), which saw him collaborating with Slater for the first time, and most famously *The Night Mail* (1936). The percussive chug of his backdrop for Auden's chanted poem about post is reminiscent of *Grimes* in its attempt to simultaneously sound like, and sound like something more than, its subject (in this case a train, rather than the sea) and in the way its grimy orchestration suddenly opens up into a shimmering dawn – a trick Britten would repeat in other operas too, such as the reveal of 'the view' from Aschenbach's hotel room in *Death in Venice*. He worked with Slater again on the Left Theatre's production of *Easter 1916*, then wrote 'generic fanfares and banquet music, which he would take to a new level eighteen years later in *Gloriana*' (Kildea, 115) for the Group Theatre's production of *Timon of Athens*. Then came the Group's *The Ascent of F6*, noteworthy 'not least for its first scene, in which the mountain-climbing hero Michael Ransom (inspired by T.E. Lawrence) is depicted reading Dante, a prototype Britten returned to in *Billy*

Budd'. Kildea compares Britten's arrangement of Auden's 'Funeral Blues' for this production to a 'Brechtian torch song' (Kildea, 125).

Exile in America meant fewer opportunities for this multidisciplinary apprenticeship to continue, although Britten and Auden were soon reunited, working together on the operetta *Paul Bunyan*, which premiered in 1941. It provides a cautionary case-study of the difficulties of crowbarring ideas from other forms into a work of music-theatre. One review called it 'a little bit of everything, a little of symbolism and uplift, a bit of socialism and of modern satire, and gags and jokes of a Hollywood sort, or of rather cheap musical comedy' (Kildea, 179–80). Auden blamed himself, 'since, at the time, I knew nothing whatsoever about opera or what is required of a librettist' (Kildea, 180). John Fuller has argued convincingly that Auden wouldn't have been the problem if he'd had 'Isherwood to rely on – the "cool-headed play doctor ... making viable constructions out of the fertile mess that Auden provided"' (Kildea, 180). Still, the operetta represented further evidence that Britten was an opera-maker waiting to happen. As Serge Koussevitsky, the director of the Boston Symphony Orchestra who commissioned *Peter Grimes* in memory of his wife, put it, how was it 'possible that such a dramatic composer had yet to write an opera?' (cited in Kildea, 196). Britten unsuccessfully attempted to recruit the 'play doctor' for his own purposes when he started work on *Grimes*, but 'the ultimate lesson of *Paul Bunyan*' – that 'fiction shaped opera, and opera shaped fiction. But in both ... plot was paramount' (Kildea, 182) – turned out to be medicine enough.

Britten composed so much music for film and theatre in the decade before *Grimes* that it's become an established critical trope to point out ways in which the work integrates theatrical soundscapes and cinematic effects. Unlike the evolutions of *Grimes* that were the product of ensemble creativity, and which can therefore often be tracked via correspondence, the presence of film and theatre music in the opera is mostly the product of Britten's private practice. The corresponding criticism feels more than usually speculative, leaning towards either the general or the very specific. Mitchell describes

> Britten's brilliant apprenticeship, the enabling creative history without which *Peter Grimes* would simply not have been possible ... the mass of dramatic music generated by Britten's association with documentary film (principally), the theatre (the Group Theatre, but not exclusively), and radio. It was in all of those potent areas ... that the youthful Britten was trained to be the 'born' opera composer.
>
> (Mitchell in Banks, 126)

This is echoed by everyone from Leonard Thompson, who played the part of Peter's apprentice in 1945 and much later wrote to Crozier that he'd come to 'think of [the opera] in cinematic terms' (23 November 1990), to Kildea, who asserts that 'certain cinematic techniques ... crept into his operas'.[7] Mitchell is braver: 'if one were looking for direct anticipations of *Grimes*, they are to be found ... in a film score from 1936, in music for a radio drama from 1943 and ... in a setting of a French folk song from 1942' (Mitchell in Banks, 129). *Love from a Stranger*, a schlocky Hitchcock-ish thriller starring a supercharged Basil Rathbone, quickly makes it clear where Mitchell is coming from: the title credits are accompanied by music with a striking resemblance to the storm interlude of *Grimes* that, by fading into a London where it's 'raining cats and dogs' while also foreshadowing Rathbone's character's explosive psychosis, plays a similar double-role to much of the weather music in *Grimes*.

For me, the most interesting thing about Britten's work on *Love from a Stranger* is its fluid transitions from diegetic sound – music which is actually present in the fictional world of a scene, in a nightclub, say – into non-diegetic soundtrack music that plays a cinematic role, accelerating the passing of time or progress through a montage of locations. This is a trick whose adoption within theatre feels pretty recent, but which Britten deploys brilliantly in *Grimes*, for example with the church music and sung prayers that become a gothic commentary on Peter and Ellen's duet about their future together, at the beginning of Act 2. But diegetic sound is only one strand of the not-conventionally operatic music in *Peter Grimes*, much of which could, arguably, be comfortably accommodated into twenty-first-century multimedia theatre, and might therefore be considered evidence of the impact of Britten's multidisciplinary apprenticeship on his subsequent opera-making.

There are the interludes, six soundscapes whose effect is half Bernstein-esque dance intermission, half so cinematic they were actually turned into films by video artist Tal Rosner (Figure 3), who reconfigured their emphasis towards bridges, cityscapes and abstract industrial geometry representative of their structural role in the opera. Then there are the considerable number of occasions when music is playing or people are singing: the chorus's refrain as they go about their daily routine at the beginning of Act 1 and the end of Act 3, the 'Old Joe has gone fishing' sing-song in the pub at the end of Act 1, the liturgy sung by congregation, choir and Rector at the beginning of Act 2, the posse's marching song later

Figure 3 Still from *Four Sea Interludes*, produced for the Los Angeles Philharmonic (2015). Photograph: Kristen Loken, courtesy of Tal Rosner.

in that scene, and the dance band at the beginning of Act 3. There's also the music of cinematic effect, from the almost *Tom and Jerry*-ish sarcastic edge underscoring the Prologue, interrupted by the leitmotif of strings that transports Peter back in time to 'That evil day! / … With a childish death' (Britten, 42); to the dissonant woodwind and violins which announce the arrival of spirits in Acts 2 and 3. And floating between these categories there's the sound of the spirits themselves, a ghost chorus of 'voices' that repeat Peter's name in the opera's final scene.

This is not to say that all instrumental or unconventional music in the opera is straightforwardly theatrical: Kildea has highlighted the way Britten's use of a Passacaglia echoes the operas of Purcell (Kildea, 262), and it is conspicuous how much this attempt to plait disparate threads of the score into a Baroque curiosity feels less appropriate for the purposes of theatre than the other interludes (although I will attempt a theatrical interpretation in the next chapter). But there's an awful lot of music here that can't be contained by Kerman's model of how composition contributes to operatic drama, which he basically boils down to a three-way choice between characterisation, articulating time or imbuing atmosphere.

Diegetic and cinematic music wasn't the only product of the theatre-making that created *Peter Grimes*. Viewed through the lens of the revolution that was to come with the Angry Young Men's (and women's, such as Shelagh Delaney's) 'kitchen sink realism', many of Britten's and Slater's decisions make more sense in the context of realistic theatre than they do in opera, a form that had never before seriously engaged with this mode. This was inevitable from the moment Britten chose his source: as Crozier put it, 'in basing their opera on [Crabbe's] poem, the composer and librettist have broken away from the romantic scenes and heroic situations of operatic fashion, setting their action and their people in a homelier native background' (Crozier in Banks, 51), a defining feature I will address in the next chapter. But it's also evident in one of the constitutive operatic strands of *Grimes*, its recitative. Slater wrote, in the introduction to *Peter Grimes and Other Poems*, that the verse form he chose

> is a four-stress line with rough rhymes for the body of the drama, though I used a variety of metres for the set numbers. (The prologue is in prose.) The departure from the five-stress line which, whether in rhyming or blank

verse, has been traditional for so long in English poetic drama, was inspired by the feeling that the rotundity of five-stress verse is out of key with contemporary modes of thought and speech.

(Slater, 7)

As ever, Slater's eye was on theatre rather than opera:

A four-stress line can have a conversational rhythm, but it demands rhyming couplets. Fortunately our ears have become re-accustomed to assonance and consonantal rhyme, and by their use it is possible to use this rhythm with a sense of naturalness. Indeed I believe the return of rough rhyme is likely to help the return of poetic drama to the English stage.

(Slater, 7)

Which isn't what actually happened next, of course, but Britten was happy with the result: 'it doesn't embarrass me to think of these people, singing, & singing in English,' he wrote in a letter (cited in Banks, 27).

What did happen in the years after *Grimes*'s premiere relates to one last theatrical echo I wish to conclude with. Namely the way Britten, Pears, Crozier and Cross were so energised by the experience of working together, and so discouraged by the shortcomings of Sadler's Wells, that their not unrelated decision to found the English Opera Company could be described as the final stage of their collaboration. With its lack of permanent home and focus on agile, intimate chamber opera, it resembled a theatre ensemble far more than it did the big opera companies and festivals of the day. Although that would come later, of course, when Britten

brought world-class music to the little town, and surrounding countryside, that had furnished him with a setting with
which to announce his greatness.

Notes

1 'It may take years for an idea to get into the rehearsal room, and
   before it does it has been batted back and forth between the directors, reshaped and presented to producers and other collaborators.
   It was been presented to a writer, too, who may be engaged to
   create a full draft for the first day of rehearsal. That script becomes
   the launch pad and inspiration for most of the devising process'
   (Graham and Hoggett, 5).
2 Early drafts of scenes in Pears's hand also reveal he had, at this
   stage, a tin ear for libretto. He'd evidently improved by 1960,
   which saw the premiere of *A Midsummer Night's Dream*, which he
   co-wrote with Britten (see L5 and L7 in Banks, 60).
3 For Nick Clark, the librarian at the Britten-Pears Archive, it
   was Britten's collaborations with Myfanwy Piper: in his view,
   which he expressed during one of my research visits, only she
   achieved the right balance with Britten, not throwing projects
   at him all the time, leaving him space, accepting his suggestions
   but also maintaining distance and integrity.
4 It was striking how much heavy lifting, in terms of direction and
   design, was required to drag Fiona Shaw's 2015 Glyndebourne
   production of *The Rape of Lucretia* into theatrically interesting territory: 'She dispenses with the idea that the Male and Female
   Choruses (Allan Clayton and Kate Royal) should be detached
   from the action and reimagines them as a pair of archeologists,
   themselves traumatised by war, who piece the opera's narrative
   together from what they unearth during a dig, and whose relationship and beliefs are challenged by what they find. The concept
   allows Shaw to probe both the work's unstable mix of pagan bru-
   tality and Christian moralising, and its sometimes troubling sexual
   politics' (*Gramophone*).
5 A *British Theatre* review of *The Cocktail Party* described 'elec-
   tronically adjusted cocktail-bar piano music, both sophisticated

and edgy' (23 September 2015), while Lyn Gardner wrote, of *An Inspector Calls*, that 'the actors play second fiddle in a production that, from Stephen Warbeck's doomy music to Rick Fisher's eerie lighting, magically reinvents a middlebrow drama and transforms it into thrilling and pertinent theatre' (*Guardian*, 13 November 2016).

6 On '*The Duchess of Malfi*, Brecht and W.H. Auden's adaptation of Webster's play, for which Britten was writing music' (Kildea, 278); sadly, the score is lost, although we know it included settings for songs taken from *The White Devil*, also by Webster.

7 Kildea's examples include *Billy Budd* ('a cinematic fade from one scene and era to another') and *Gloriana*, which utilises, he suggests, cinema-esque flashbacks (Kildea, 109).

the putrid and fissile geography around Aldeburgh; to use the landscape, in fact, to amplify certain energies and expand the world of his poem into more metaphysical territory. Britten's and Slater's writing is located in a strikingly similar place, 'full of respect for Crabbe'; their protagonist might not be 'quite the Peter Grimes of Crabbe' but their opera is made of the same stuff as the *Peter Grimes* section of Crabbe. Indeed, the opera's extrapolation of this part of Crabbe's project through music, libretto and theatrical tableaux, forming a proto-psychogeographical framework with which to make sense of post-war consciousness and resituate post-war English art, is the beating heart of *Peter Grimes*'s claim to be a great work.

'It is a bleak little place; not beautiful,' wrote Forster in the programme notes for the first production (Forster in Britten, 15). 'The scenery becomes melancholy and flat; expanses of mud, saltish commons, the marsh-birds crying. Crabbe heard that sound and saw that melancholy and they got into his verse' (Forster in Britten, 15). This text was an abridged version of the *Listener* article that dragged Britten back across the sea to his home county, a transatlantic take on the same journey that brought a reluctant Crabbe back to Aldeburgh in 1809 to finish *The Borough*, which was published the next year. 'The estuaries … smell powerful and, at low tide, putrid', writes Kevin Crossley-Holland in his own introduction to Crabbe's verse, but these 'unlovely, humdrum aspects of the place … barb locals … and never let them go' (Crossley-Holland, 7). Crabbe

> escaped from Aldeburgh as soon as he could … Yet he never escaped from Aldeburgh in the spirit, and it was the making of him as a poet. Even when he was writing

of other things, there steals again and again into his verse the sea, the estuary, the flat Suffolk coast, local meannesses, and an odour of brine and dirt.

(Forster in Britten, 15)

It's tempting to think that, as the 22nd of *The Borough*'s 24 letters, Crabbe was writing 'Letter XXII' during his 1809 visit, and that's why it contains such a visceral account of Forster's and Crossley-Holland's melancholy, putrid coastline:

> The bounding marsh-bank and the blighted tree;
> The water only, when the tides were high,
> When low, the mud half cover'd and half-dry;
> The sun-burnt tar that blisters on the planks,
> And bank-side stakes in their uneven ranks;
> … He [Peter] nursed the feelings these dull scenes
>   produce,
> And loved to stop beside the opening sluice;
> Where the small stream, confined in narrow bound,
> Ran with a dull, unvaried, sadd'ning sound;
> Where all, presented to the eye or ear,
> Oppress'd the soul with misery, grief and fear.
>
> (Crabbe in Crabbe, Heber and Pollok, 128)

Nature forms something like a graveyard, here, with its ranks of stakes; a 'no-man's land, which never belongs to earth or sea entirely' (Crossley-Holland, 7). Neither critic of Crabbe's nature writing is quite willing to follow the metaphor through, though, to the logical if metaphysical end-point of this cocktail of putrefaction and liminal entrapment: that what is formed is a kind of purgatory, where souls are tangled up with the fishing nets, and the dead interact with the living. Which is odd, because Crabbe states clearly that the spirits which emerge out of his poem, shaking their 'hoary locks' (Crabbe in Crabbe, Heber and Pollok, 129) in the traditional literary manner established by *Macbeth*, do so in the surrounding landscape rather than the cobbled streets of the Borough: 'There were three places, where they ever rose … / Places accursed, where, if a man remain, / He'll see the things which strike him to the brain' (Crabbe in Crabbe, Heber and Pollok, 130).

It is this anti-pastoral, sadomasochistic, spiritualist depiction of the English far east, at stark odds with the late Georgian house style of 'happy shepherds and shepherdesses, who were always dancing, and anyhow had hearts of gold' (Forster in Britten, 15), which justifies the use of an apparent anachronism like 'psychogeography' to describe verse published twelve years before the birth of Baudelaire. Equally pioneering, though, was the fact Crabbe wrote about this section of shoreline at all. It would take a century and a half for English literature to catch up: I've heard it theorised that the East Anglian coast was neglected by imaginative writing about the sea for the entire period between Crabbe and Britten. No doubt this overstates the situation: if Constable, the artists of the Norwich School, Turner, Philip Wilson Steer, John Nash and Stanley Spencer were able to keep the flame of Suffolk painting alive over the same period, albeit with a primarily inland focus, there must have been some authors too. But the loose Eng Lit chain that can be traced along the coast-line at the bottom of the British Isles does appear to stop, rather abruptly, at the Thames Estuary: from Dylan Thomas's South Wales, the setting for *Under Milk Wood*, a project created out of strikingly similar component parts to Crabbe's poem; through to John Cowper Powys's and Hardy's Wessex, then

Woolf's and du Maurier's Cornwall; and beyond that Jane Austen's Sussex (via Dorset) and Dickens's Kent.[3]

It is harder to connect the music about the sea from the same period to specific locations (a curiosity that in itself says something about Britten's originality). While both Debussy's *La mer* and Frank Bridge's *The Sea* are indelibly associated with Eastbourne in Sussex, and Bax's Tintagel reveals its Cornish connection in the title, Stanford's *Songs of the Sea*, Elgar's *Sea Pictures* and Vaughan-Williams's *Sea Symphony* are all based on texts that confuse the geography somewhat: while Stanford's lean towards Devon, Vaughan-Williams set verse from the American poet Walt Whitman's *Leaves of Grass*. What can be stated confidently is that neither composers nor writers were regularly turning to the landscape of East Suffolk for inspiration. But once Britten and Slater had rearticulated Crabbe's landscape as a place to confront twentieth-century demons, as well as pre-Victorian ones, the sluice gates opened. With this one wildly influential opera, and the festival that only came to exist because of a chain of events set off by that first production of *Grimes*, Britten and Slater catalysed a renaissance that meant cultural production in the second half of the twentieth century became disproportionally obsessed with Crabbe's coastline.

From Ronald Blythe's *Akenfield* (1969) to Penelope Fitzgerald's *The Bookshop* (1978), and from W.G. Sebald's *Rings of Saturn* (1995) to Robert Macfarlane's libretto about Orford Ness, *Untrue Island* (2012), there's a rich vein of postwar East Anglian literature, underpinned by biographical connections, many of which can be traced back to Britten. In 1955 Blythe was made the administrative assistant of the fledgling Aldeburgh Festival, a period he recalled in his 2013 book *The Time by the Sea* (Britten was supposed to return the favour by composing the music for Peter Hall's film of *Akenfield*, but was prevented from doing so by a heart attack). Fitzgerald 'went to the second night of Benjamin Britten's *Peter Grimes* at Sadler's Wells, wearing a new black chiffon blouse, and was excited enough by it to … keep her programme all her life' (Lee, 92). Sebald seems to have had little interest in Britten – he avoided Aldeburgh on the walk he documents in *Rings of Saturn*, perhaps considering it to be, by then, too obvious a staging post – but Sebald's work has been an important point of reference for Macfarlane throughout his career.[4] And Macfarlane brings us back around to Britten by revealing that his inspirations for *Untrue Island* were 'the Kevin Flanagan Quartet's settings of Gary Snyder's Rip-rap poems, the Richard Burton reading of Dylan Thomas's *Under Milk Wood*, and Benjamin Britten's opera *Peter Grimes*' (*Guardian*, 8 July 2012).

Each of these texts echoes Britten's and Slater's and Crabbe's characterisation of a decaying, slippery, magnetic, supernatural Suffolk. 'Listen now, listen back to the pasts of the Ness, which speak, and speak, and speak of loss', urges Macfarlane's libretto. On that strip of saltmarsh, a couple of miles downcoast from Aldeburgh, the sand and shingle are 'in continual migration, forming and reforming their shape as they shift' and revealing 'the bones of ancient men' (*Guardian*, 8 July 2012). Fitzgerald's Hardborough, a hardly disguised Southwold, a little further upcoast, is likewise

> an island between sea and river, muttering and drawing into itself as soon as it felt the cold. Every fifty years or so it had lost, as though careless or indifferent to such things, another means of communication.
>
> (Fitzgerald, 8)

This liminal isolation results in a town 'infested by a poltergeist', and thanks to its *'unusual period atmosphere'* (Fitzgerald, 14, her italics) the lines between sanity and lunacy blur: 'The word in Hardborough for "mad" was "not quite right"' (Fitzgerald, 15). In *Akenfield*, 'the villager is imprisoned by the sheer implacability of the "everlasting circle"' (Blythe, *Akenfield*, 15), a purgatory evoked, in Hall's 1974 film, by a scene (Figure 4) in which the protagonist sees the ghost of his own grandfather, played by the same actor, and yoked to the same constraints that have kept three generations in the tiny universe of the village. And when Sebald reaches the cliffs of Covehithe, a couple more miles upcoast from Southwold, he witnesses a scene from hell itself:

> I crouched down and, overcome by a sudden panic, looked over the edge. A couple lay down there, in the bottom of the pit, as I thought: a man stretched full length over another body of which nothing was visible but the legs spread and angled. In the startled moment when this image went through me, which lasted an eternity, it seemed as if the man's feet twitched like those of one just hanged.
>
> (Sebald, 43)

What's most remarkable about this geographical and atmospheric consistency is the variety of the subject matter these four authors have sought to articulate and amplify by situating their stories within it. In *Akenfield*, it's an agricultural way of life that will soon be gone forever, but which still exerts a powerful charge. *Untrue Island* and the *Rings of Saturn* both oscillate between sweeping environmental themes and specific episodes of human violence, from the persecution of the Serbs in the

Figure 4 Stills from the last scene of *Akenfield*, directed by Peter Hall (Angle Films Limited, 1974).

Second World War which Sebald considers at the Crown Hotel in Southwold, to the 'bomb buildings' (*Guardian*, 8 July 2012) of Orford Ness, where weapons and technology for both World Wars and the Cold War were tested throughout the twentieth century. Meanwhile *The Bookshop* tells a smaller, familiar-sounding tale of aspiration and survival in a seaside town.

Whether or not *Peter Grimes* is directly responsible for the existence and tonal consistency of this slightly random sample of works isn't really the point. They simply amount to the most interesting part of a story that, because of the Aldeburgh Festival, and the waves of commissioning and cultural community-building (or, to put it another way, gentrification) that have been its gift to East Suffolk, is to some extent self-evident. The second half of the twentieth century, that is to say the decades after *Grimes*, saw a significant easterly swerve in music, literature and art, which continues to produce work that engages intensely with the coastline, from Maggi Hambling's *Scallop* to Blake Morrison's *Shingle Street*. Sarah Lucas even moved into a house Britten once owned. Such is the impact of a great work. In fact the only major art form that doesn't seem to have benefited much from the Suffolk renaissance that began with *Peter Grimes* is theatre. I wonder why.

Britten's and Slater's extrapolation of Crabbe's nature writing adopts four elemental shapes, each of which is formed out of the fabric of theatre as well as music to an extent that means it is reasonable to describe each as *a theatre*, within an opera.

A theatre of sea

It need hardly be stated that *Peter Grimes* is an artwork about the sea. Many people's first encounter with the opera is through its Sea Interludes, whose ubiquity exceeds that of the full work because of the quality that is so often the basis of an extract becoming famous in its own right: they are mimetic and naturalistic, insofar as music can be either of those things. In the first, third and fifth interludes one hears, or feels one hears, the cry of the gull and the even breaths of a flint-grey sea rolling into the shingle. After watching Rosner's images of bridges and cityscapes, I felt compelled to walk the length of Aldeburgh beach, humming Interlude V under my breath, to return it to its natural place. The danger of this powerful, literal connection between music and landscape is that it might fool an audience into thinking that the sea's contribution to *Peter Grimes* is limited to a picturesque setting, or maybe just a rich seam of metaphor: 'What harbour shelters peace? / Away from tidal waves, away from storms, / What harbour can embrace / Terrors and tragedies?' (42). But actually, its most important role in the drama is as an active character, rather than a passive context – as the opera's antagonist, perhaps. Its purpose is twofold: to besiege and isolate the Borough, and to act as a kind of siren powerful enough to turn Peter mad before tempting him into its depths and killing him.

Both parts of the characterisation are made explicit early on. In the Prologue, Peter reveals that his first apprentice died because of the irresistible attractions of the sea, which provided 'a huge catch, too big to sell here' – but as it giveth so it taketh away and William Spode died, 'lying there among the fish' (35). Then in the lines from Crabbe that the Chorus sings at the beginning of Act 1, we are warned in the following terms:

And if the springtide eats the land again,
Till even the cottages and cobbled walls of fishermen

Are billets for the thieving waves which take
As if in sleep, thieving for thieving's sake.

(38)

In other words, contrary to Ned Keene's assertion, the sea
won't hesitate in drowning your conscience as well as flooding
your kitchen. The warning is reasserted throughout the rest
of the opera, in Ned's and Hobson's reports during the storm,
for example, that 'the cliff is down / up by Grimes's hut' (44)
and 'the bridge is down' (46), and in a passage that makes us
wonder whether Peter really can 'see the shoals to which the
rest are blind' (48) or whether he's hallucinating: 'The whole
sea's boiling! / ... I'll fish the sea dry, / Flood the market. /
... Get money to choke / Down rumour's throat' (52). But
it goes beyond the text. Both ideas are entrenched through
theatrical tableaux that utilise – without being completely
dependent on – Britten's composition.

We are not simply told that the town has been cut
off: we're shown it, when Hobson, Ellen and Peter's new
apprentice enter the Boar 'soaking, muddy and bedraggled'
(46), bringing with them grim elemental reality at odds
with Balstrode's attempt to start a song 'for peace sake' (45).
'Old Joe has gone fishing', one of those important examples
of music adopting a form that is as much theatrical as it is
operatic, a drinking song, has itself been a dialogue between
the sea as giver and as taker. Peter 'breaks the round' (46),
pulling apart its careful construction with a dire invocation
and a different time signature: 'We found us Davy Jones. /
Bring him in with horror! Bring him in with terror! And
bring him in with sorrow!' (46). Similarly, the fact that the
'cliff is down' is proven theatrically in the next act, with a
precisely outlined dumbshow that plays out to the sound

of Britten at his most blatantly cinematic, with a flurry of strings and a scream:

> There is a knocking at the other door. Peter turns towards it, then retreats. Meanwhile the boy climbs out. When Peter is between the two doors the boy screams and falls out of sight. Peter runs to the cliff door, feels for his grip and then swings after him.
>
> (53)

And as the sea consumes Peter at the end – 'Old Davy Jones shall answer: / Come home, come home' (58) – we are presented with another concentration of theatrical rather than operatic activity. Balstrode's final words are spoken, rather than sung, and Peter's boat slips into the sea in silence, before 'the cue for the orchestra to return' (58). A reprise of Interlude I accompanies the longest stage direction of the opera, a full seven paragraphs of stage business. And to return to those interludes, if the sea is a siren, doesn't that mean those orchestral passages might be interpreted as something more than moody descriptions? Can we start to hear them as one half of a seductive theatrical dialogue calling Peter back, back into the sea?

A theatre of sky

The sky also provides *Grimes* with a steady supply of symbolism, most prominently in Peter's pivotal aria, in which the clouds and behind them the stars represent destiny in the traditional manner: 'As the sky turns, the world for us to change' (45). And the sky's place in the opera is also defined, initially, by the interludes, which are as much a representation of the time of day, the light and the weather, as they are the sound of the waves: when Interludes I, II, III and V were published separately as an orchestral suite, Britten titled them Dawn, Storm, Sunday Morning and Moonlight respectively. But, like the sea, these passive musical origins are quickly superseded by an active theatrical role. If the sea is Britten's and Slater's antagonist, then the sky is the opera's engine; very little would happen if it wasn't for the weather. Or rather, the 'undramatic, unhurrying and unending' (Crozier in Banks, 19, the final words of his production notes) everyday routine, the 'everlasting circle' that is described by the Chorus at the beginning of Act 1, and reprised at the end of Act 3, would continue without much interruption if it wasn't for three interventions by the sky which either catalyse action or recalibrate the atmosphere onstage: the storm of Act 1, the bright optimistic morning of Act 2 and the eerie summer fog in Act 3.

It is the gale that lights the touch paper of the opera. Balstrode sees 'the storm cone' (41) through his glass and the petty domestic back and forth of the first part of Act 1 – the 'good morning!' (39) exchanges are reminiscent of nothing so much as a Disney film – are blasted out of the way by deep swelling brass, the forceful Balstrode baritone and a hysterical Chorus split along gender lines, all of which are rather more representative of what's to come. But the impact of the storm is felt choreographically too, in the manner Crozier hinted at with his note about 'the crowd [as] vital element'. A trope is established when the collective cry of 'spare our coast!' is followed by a sudden 'General Exeunt – mostly through the swing doors of the Boar' (41), leaving Peter 'leaning against the wind' (42), namely that, after Interlude II, the storm will play out through a dynamic sequence of entries and exits. The recitative inside the Boar is musically pedestrian, dominated by

Figure 5 Still from Act 1 Scene 2 in the ENO Screen trailer for the 2014 revival of the ENO's 2009 production of *Peter Grimes*, directed by David Alden.

the chirruping fears of the Nieces, and Auntie's and Balstrode's didacticism. It's permitted to swing back towards the elemental intensity of the interlude only when somebody crashes through the door, 'with disastrous consequences. A sudden gust howls through the door, the shutters of the window fly open, a pane blown in' (43). These flashing switches from interior to exterior are often one of the most actively *directed* scenes in the opera. When the door opened in the ENO's *Grimes*, everyone in the pub pitched from one side to the other, as though on a ship in a storm (Figure 5). The most dramatic moment of all is silent, however: the stage direction for Peter's entrance doesn't mention a 'struggle with the wind'. The contrast between the repeated single note of Peter's aria and the orchestral tumult of the storm might be the opera's purest expression of Britten's compositional vision, but that doesn't mean it's not also framed by carefully considered choreography.

The other two changes in the weather are more subtle, but the atmospheric shifts they accompany are significant: the 'glitter of sunlight' that bids Ellen 'rejoice / And lift our hearts on high' (47) at the beginning of Act 2, before Peter brings her crashing back to earth; and the 'cloud-swept moon' and 'distant fog-horn' that create an atmosphere[5] within which the mad fisherman can communicate with his 'voices' (57). It's not a coincidence that much of the music in both scenes could be as straightforwardly integrated into a layered, multimedia theatre – of bells and prayers and the sound of spirits – as it could into conventional operatic tableaux.

A theatre of earth

If the sea is *Peter Grimes*'s antagonist, and the weather is its engine, then its representation of the land defines the work's dimensions, the space between its three worlds: the sea, the Borough and a surrounding landscape of 'shore, / The marsh, the fields' (57). Again, a strand of metaphor, here symbolising a depth of identity and belonging at odds with the shallow Borough, disguises this more dynamic role. 'I am native, rooted here', cries Peter – a line that appeared on all the publicity materials for *Grimes on the Beach* – before offering a concise account of Crabbe's 'dull views':

> By familiar fields
> Marsh and sand,
> Ordinary streets,
> Prevailing wind.

(41)

It's the opera's *theatre* of earth that entrenches Peter's outsider status, though, by precisely delineating the distance between the landscape around his hut and the Borough.

There's a palpable sense, by the end of Act 1, that the apprentice's new home with Peter is located far away from the relative warmth of the Boar. 'Your hut's washed away,' warns Auntie; 'Only the cliff' (46), replies Peter, as if it's a small thing. And the act ends with a rhetorical question sung by the entire cast, except Peter and Ellen: 'Home? Do you call that home?' (46). How then to convey this sense of Peter's world as a terrifying otherscape? Through set, certainly: Peter's hut makes a mockery of the naturalism Britten supposedly preferred, converting Crabbe's 'mud-wall'd hovel' (Crabbe in Crabbe, Heber and Pollok, 52) into an almost comically Expressionist 'upturned boat … bare and forbidding'. But also through the time it takes to get there. *Peter Grimes* is an opera full of rapid accelerations of plot – most dramatically in chorus scenes, such as when reactionary posses are formed in Acts 2 and 3 – with a timeframe that skips ambiguously between acts. Its one and only moment of something like real-time action occurs between the posse's departure for Grimes's hut and its arrival after a considerable interval, which has been filled with the women's quartet, the Passacaglia and Peter's reflection on a future that might have been.

This passage begins with another moment of not necessarily operatic music, inserted by Slater: the posse's marching song, sung to the beat of a drum. It fades out as the chorus leaves the stage – or, in the case of *Grimes on the Beach*, literally marched away towards the real-life sea. It also feels deliberately topographical, shifting down a key every few lines. This interpretation is confirmed when the posse returns,

their volume and pitch now rising – 'the song of the neighbours coming up the hill' (53) – as Peter riffs on their melody a full octave higher. 'Neighbours' is somewhat deceptive,
though, because it's taken them quite a while to arrive, during which time the landscape has been coloured in by the
Passacaglia. This more ambiguous interlude has been interpreted in a number of ways, from Kildea's sense of time
passing, to Darrell Handel's tracing of 'the derangement of
Grimes' (*Tempo*, October 1970). Others have translated the
sound of the viola as Britten's attempt to give the apprentice a voice: what Mitchell calls 'the impersonation of the
boy' (Mitchell in Banks, 163), or perhaps his funeral march,
in the sombre passacaglia tradition. If we listen to it as a con-
tinuation of the mimetic, naturalistic, ecological project of the
Sea Interludes, though, I think we hear something that, with
its plodding spurts of low brass, tuning chords of trumpet
and dreamscape of chromatic xylophone, deviates in a manner that is best described as *earthy*. Is this Britten engaging
with the 'hot slimy channel' (Crabbe in Crabbe, Heber and
Pollok, 128) of Crabbe's landscape, for the first time, in order
to establish a gulf between Peter and his peers that won't now
ever be crossed?

A theatre of fire

The fourth elemental manifestation of *Peter Grimes*'s theatre
of nature is a protagonist with 'fiery visions' (42), through
whom Britten and Slater make like Crabbe and open up
a gateway between the East Suffolk landscape and more
metaphysical planes. Indeed, Peter *is* the portal: as he's
turned mad, spirits rise to the surface, before sinking back
into the swamp as Peter returns his body to the sea. *Grimes*

provides plenty of hints that there is something demonic about Peter's obsession with his craft; that he is a kind of Green Man, perhaps even a merman. We hear it as early as the Prologue, when the sarcastically percussive intonation of Swallow melts into a leitmotif of strings as Peter steps 'into the box' (35), which then find its full expression in the Sea Interludes. Then Boles calls him a 'lost soul of a fisherman' (39) and his subsequent entrance into the Boar causes another hypocritical Christian, Mrs Sedley, to faint: 'Unlike the rest he wears no oilskins. His hair looks wild' (45). His aria is charged with dramatic irony in a manner reminiscent of Caliban's 'the isle is full of noises' speech from *The Tempest*,[6] in that its crystalline truth is immediately clear to the audience but unrecognised by the characters onstage. We can't help but become complicit. Boles responds with more accusations and Peter drags the metaphysical framework of the scene down into Davy Jones's locker, just as the next character in the opera who is to die, the apprentice, enters the room.

By Act 2, Peter's journey from aspirational 'wealthy merchant / Grimes' (42) to the devil with 'glitter in his eyes' (49), whose only exercise is violence, is almost complete. As his last vision of civilised domesticity – 'Fruit in the garden, children by the shore' (52) – collapses under the weight of his guilt and paranoia, supernatural forces start to creep through the fissures in his consciousness, announcing themselves with a schlocky trill of shrilly dissonant woodwind:

> Sometimes I see that boy here in this hut.
> He's there now, I can see him, he is there!
> His eyes are on me as they were that evil day.
>
> (52)

This is echoed in Interlude VI, in the next act, which repeats the trick with a flurry of high-tension strings which work themselves up to an unbearable, Bernard Hermann-ish pitch, cut off with a tambourine splash. The resulting tableau immediately establishes contrast with the concrete realities of the previous manhunt. 'As before we can hear shouting, now in the far distance' (57), but that distance is defined by something other than landscape, because the disembodied 'Voices' (not 'Chorus') behave very differently to the posse of Act 2. They maintain an uncannily even tone that drifts in and out of the scene, apparently randomly and then suddenly more urgently, at a different pitch here, a different volume there, less music than polyphonic effect. Peter is interacting with the ghosts of his past and future, 'the first one died, just died … / The other slipped, and died … / And the third will …' before he returns 'home', to 'Old Davy Jones' (57). And he is doing so 'alone by his boat in the changeful light of a cloud-swept moon' (58), just as it is in 'the mid stream' where 'the spirits rise' in Crabbe: 'through the water came / A hollow groan' (129).

There is, of course, a noble tradition of mad scenes in the theatre, such as those of Ophelia and Lear which are likewise rooted in natural imagery: the former's 'fennel for you, and columbines' (Act 4, Scene 5), and the latter's 'tempest in my mind' (Act 3, Scene 4).[7] Peter's is seemingly made of similar stuff: a patchwork of reprised lines, snatches of song and occasional 'method in 't'. But it also goes further than most mad scenes insofar as it encourages an audience to hear more than just method, and to actually believe in its phantoms as much as in any of the wider fantasy. By making Peter's ghosts answer back, to us as well as his protagonist, Britten gave Crabbe's spirit world substance, and established an energy with which

Fitzgerald and Sebald could do the same. And he did so in a scene that was wrought out of dynamic theatrical collaboration, this time with Duncan.

My intention is not to suggest that there is only one way to read, listen to and watch *Peter Grimes* which reveals its Great Work status, and that is as a geographical and psycho-geographical opera/play. As with all major artworks there is an infinite variety of readings to impose on Britten's and Slater's work, which it is capable of standing up to; in fact, Britten's own interpretation of the opera evolved as he got older, cleaving to a neater biographical parallel than was, as far as Kildea is concerned, necessarily intended at the time of writing (Kildea, 3). Rather, my argument is that, regardless of the emphasis of the interpretation, *Grimes*'s characterisation, dynamics and dimensions are almost as dependent on a distinctive depiction of the East Suffolk landscape as they are on Slater's words and Britten's music. Crabbe's coastline is woven into the fabric of the opera so much more tightly than its other preoccupations that these emerge *out of* the representation of landscape, rather than alongside. Take the three most established interpretations: *Grimes* as biographical-pacifist, as biographical-queer and as socialist artwork. If Peter's rejection represents Britten, Pears, Auden *et al.*'s exile across the Atlantic during the Second World War, that only amplifies the significance of the sea. And if the way Peter is drawn by that rejection towards catastrophic homosocial situations is to be interpreted as a reflection on, or of, Britten's and Pears's closeted homosexuality, then the fact Peter's repressed feelings manifest themselves throughout in natural and supernatural metaphor only becomes more central to the drama.[8] As for readings which find a parable of failing capitalist aspiration within a community entirely lacking in socialist solidarity – well, such a story still depends on a natural resource and a means of production at the mercy of sea and sky, and therefore has to trace a narrative of eco-Marxism, rather than any other kind.

Strip the landscape out of *Peter Grimes* and you won't be left with much. Frame it front and centre, though, in an unmediated form – Aldeburgh's actual beach, say, on a summer evening like the one in Act 3 – and its unlovely but astonishing theatre of place will be unleashed. It won't matter if the wind is blowing in the wrong direction, and you can't hear every second note, or third word. You'll still find a great work, only this one will look an awful lot like a play.

Notes

1 Curiously another adaptation of the story, by Andrew Beattie, was staged at Eltham College, a different school just a couple of miles away from Crown Wood, in 1998.

2 Ironically, before the poorhouse's part in the history of Framlingham Castle was rediscovered by English Heritage, Britten approached the custodians of the site about using it as an Aldeburgh Festival venue. It seems he was unaware that he was considering the very location where, presumably, Ned Keene found Peter's 'bargain'.

3 Admittedly Dickens did cross over into East Anglia a couple of times – in the chapters of *David Copperfield* set in Yarmouth, for example – as did Rudyard Kipling, Jean Ingelow and George Orwell. But it's not the location with which any of these writers are primarily associated.

4 In Grant Gee's film *Patience: After Sebald*, Macfarlane memorably recalls the experience of attempting the *Rings of Saturn* walk. He failed when he got to Lowestoft and, rather than reflecting on a town so close to death that 'nothing is moving' (Sebald, 68), which is what Sebald saw, instead leapt happily into the sea.

5 'The chief problem in Grimes's mad-scene is how to suggest the sea mist that has crept up around the Borough during the night', wrote Crozier in his production notes (Crozier in Banks, 19).

6 Indeed it's tempting to read the 'Great Bear' aria's last line – 'who can turn skies back and begin again?' (45) – as an explicit reference to Caliban's words: 'The clouds methought would open and show riches / Ready to drop upon me that, when I waked, / I cried to dream again' (Act 3, Scene 2).

7 'I still marvel at the fact that a composer of Britten's youth could have chosen this far from popular subject and composed … a work of almost Shakespearean dimensions,' wrote Edmund Wilson in his review of the first production of *Grimes* (Wilson, 186).

8 Kildea traces a helpful history of this most recurring reading in the prologue of his biography, from Hans Keller's 'psychosexual analysis' of *Grimes*, to Philip Brett's identification of the 'predominantly negative "homosexual vision"' at the heart of every one of Britten's operas (Kildea, 3–4).

4

'Of use to people'

'Make it like the wind, Angelo.' That was the extent of the brief David Lynch gave the composer Angelo Badalamenti when they worked together on the soundtrack for Lynch's 1986 film *Blue Velvet*. It would take another four years for this characteristically trashy-romantic, ambiguous sentiment – and the special symmetry of their collaboration – to reach full flower. Then came *Twin Peaks*, arguably Lynch's greatest work of sound and vision, and television would never be the same again.

Coverage of the series' 2017 revival revealed how much of the energy and endurance of its influence is the product of Badalamenti's score. One article in the *Guardian* asserted that 'to love *Twin Peaks* was to love Badalamenti's music', before quoting the musician Jamie Stewart (who has covered a lot of it with his band, Xiu Xiu): 'If you hum the first notes of the opening theme you're immediately transported into another world … Apart from the timpani in *2001: A Space Odyssey*, almost nothing else is as evocative' (24 March 2017). When I read this suggestion I was struck by the way it chimed with my experience of listening to *Grimes*: it's not until that first leitmotif of strings sounds, so unlike the start of the Prologue, that one suddenly understands there is something potent and truthful and strange, here, bubbling up between the operatic mannerisms. Then I realised why these two very different projects manage to conjure, and so quickly, such an eerily similar effect. Badalamenti's 'Twin Peaks Theme' continues to attract acclaim as a masterpiece of music for television capable of underpinning Lynch's 'pioneering example of unorthodox, auteur-driven event TV' (*Guardian*, 24 March 2017), but listen to it after a couple of hours spent on Britten's beach, and it starts to sound suspiciously like a synthetic rehash of a Sea Interlude.

Consider the first seven minutes of the *Twin Peaks* pilot (Figure 6), which lead up to the big reveal of Laura Palmer's lifeless face, probably the show's most iconic scene. The episode begins with a strikingly lovely credits sequence that anchors Stewart's 'first notes' in the landscape that furnishes the show with much of its magic: we see a songbird on a branch, then a sawmill against a backdrop of mountains and forest. Then as the melody opens up with a directness that is at first rather shocking and then totally convincing, the focus switches to the machinery of the mill, as representative of human interaction with nature as the Chorus singing Crabbe at the end of Interlude I. We start to understand what this cheap but affecting music might mean as the credits cut to the Twin Peaks sign (population 51,201, about to be rounded down) with its two painted mountains and the real-life peaks behind, illustrating the difference between what's true and what is uncannily idealised chimera, the tension that torques both the aesthetic and the narrative of the show. This image is held for an unusually long time, before the credits play themselves out, first with a waterfall and then a frame

Figure 6 Still from one of the opening scenes of the first episode of *Twin Peaks*, directed by David Lynch (Lynch/Frost Productions, 1990).

of gently flowing water. By this point it's become weirdly conspicuous how long this has now gone on, as the first two bars of the theme repeat themselves, again and again. In other words, these notes aren't merely transporting: they're also engaged, like *Grimes*'s Passacaglia, in the trudging work of transportation.

Then, for fewer than ten seconds, the only moment in the first five minutes when this happens, the music melts into the sounds of nature: water again, and wading birds. But with the distant and portentous sound of a foghorn, which recurs in a manner reminiscent of Act 3 Scene 2 of *Grimes*, the synthetic strings resume, and we start to appreciate that here is a place where music will play a double role: it will bring an undercurrent of discomfort and horror to the innocent scenes it accompanied in the credits; it is, like much of what we'll find in *Twin Peaks*, both a blessing and a curse.

Now, would you believe it, a *fisherman* is walking by a lake. He stops, murmurs to himself 'the lonesome foghorn blows', and sees a body on the muddy beach between water and shore. The music has swelled to a new prominence; looming, it suggests the discovery might be the source of our alarm, which we now realise has risen in time with the music. The fisherman calls the local sheriff, says 'she's dead, wrapped in plastic'. The sheriff considers his next question; a pause, then, 'where?' We don't hear the answer, but soon return to the scene, and the music is back. As the men roll the body over, it finds a major chord, and with that it starts to climb. By the time the wrapping is pulled back, it's risen by an octave. And then, just as it reaches its highest pitch, we see her: the face of a beautiful woman, kissed by water, frozen and blue and flecked with grains of silt like diamonds. The men say her name and the music resolves itself fully into 'Laura Palmer's Theme', the simple, ravishing piano melody that apparently took Badalamenti just 20 minutes to complete. '[He] suggested developing it further, but Lynch replied, "Don't change a single note. I see Twin Peaks"' (*Guardian*, 24 March 2017).

The memory of Laura's face refracts into several of the ghosts in *Twin Peaks*'s machine; it's the source of much of the show's mysterious force. And, like the spirits invoked in the first act of *Peter Grimes*, which materialise in the last, it emerges from and manifests itself in a very deliberate intersection of landscape and music: a metaphysical psychogeography of sound. As Isabella van Elferen puts it in an essay in *Popular Ghosts: The Haunted Spaces of Everyday Culture*,

> From the first camera shots observing the discovery of Laura Palmer's murdered body … the tranquil countryside atmosphere is shot through with ambiguity. The nostalgic home is by no means idyllic, but reveals itself as a borderland where life and death, ghosts and humans, good and evil, dwell side by side. The disturbing soundtrack that Angelo Badalamenti composed for the series has often been described as the most eerie film music ever. It accompanies the ghostly dimension of the series and conjures up ghosts, making them discernible even when the eye does not see them. The *Twin Peaks* spectres haunt the viewer even more than they do the characters, because Badalamenti's music gives them a ghostly voice that is often only heard by TV audiences.
>
> (van Elferen, 282)

What van Elferen sees and hears in *Twin Peaks* sounds a lot like the theatre of *Peter Grimes* I identified in the previous chapter. And this feels like a more interesting entry-point into reflection on what *Grimes* as great play might do to the canon, what the cultural-historical impact of this recharacterisation might be, than the other questions of influence and revisionism I've already posed in passing. Which is to say that sure, perhaps John Osborne's and Joan Littlewood's revolutions have different, earlier origins than theatre history usually recognises, and perhaps the Suffolk renaissance of the second half of the twentieth century can be traced back to a single source. But why stop there, when there seems to be a case for stretching the counterfactual all the way to Hollywood?

Let's speculate ambitiously, and suggest that Britten, by 1945 an established composer of film and theatre scores, drew on this experience to create a haunted soundscape half a century before Badalamenti was adulated for doing the same (by an audience that hadn't thought to look for Lynchian kicks in Britain's post-war opera scene): what might *that* mean? That Lynch and Badalamenti are derivative in a different way from all the other kitschy, referential ways we already know about? That *Twin Peaks*'s project is less Middle American than has hitherto been assumed, and is actually a regional expression of a transnational trope? That perhaps there was a more dynamic exchange, whether conscious or otherwise, between twentieth-century opera and television than is contained by a narrative defined up to now by specific crossover works, such as Robert Ashley's *Perfect Lives* (1984)? That thrilling moments of music for television like *Twin Peaks* could have happened sooner, and more variously, if directors and composers had only opened their eyes and ears and been willing to enthusiastically mine this conversation between forms? This might sound like an excessive extrapolation of the ambition I outlined at the beginning of this book – to encourage theatre-makers to recognise *Peter Grimes*, and opera more generally, as a relevant and resonant reference point for their practice – but look what happened when cinema did engage imaginatively with the structures and textures of one of Britten's operas. 'The composer part of me is still pinching itself that the music of a modern giant … was used so extensively in a major motion picture', wrote Russell Platt of Wes Anderson's *Moonrise Kingdom* (2002), which drew heavily on *Noye's Fludde*, in the *New Yorker*:

This sort of thing just isn't supposed to happen, after all ... [Anderson] 'sets' his film to Britten's opera almost in the way in which a composer 'sets' a poet's or lyricist's words in a song. Indeed, the final credits of *Moonrise Kingdom* are matched, gesture for gesture, to the sounds of the closing Fugue from another Britten masterwork, 'The Young Person's Guide to the Orchestra' ... The opera is simultaneously the movie's scaffolding and its secret life, its invisible 'color,' a mixture of innocence and sophistication that influences the film's essential style and the equal weights that adults and children have in it.

(6 August 2012)

Platt's piece ends with a quotation from a famous speech by Britten: 'going very much against the fiercely modernist élite compositional trends of 1964, [he] said that he simply wanted his music to be "of use to people"'.

But the trick hasn't been repeated, despite *Moonrise Kingdom*'s success. So how might filmmakers less literate and open-minded than Wes Anderson be switched on to the potential of opera to inform their work? Through the recognition that certain operas are plays too, of course – a form they've been comfortable borrowing from and adapting for as long as cinema has existed.

And yet. To sketch a through-line that connects *Peter Grimes* to a television show made half a century later, in the woodlands of Washington State, is to highlight the inevitable shortcomings of reassessing influence in terms of revisionism and the counterfactual. Whether small-scale (did Penelope Fitzgerald move to Southwold, and find a coastline infested with ghosts, in part because of the impact of the second night of the first production of *Grimes*?) or skipping ambitiously from Littlewood to Sebald to Lynch, what can this speculation amount to without evidence that is mostly undiscoverable? Uncharitable attempts to undercut other artists' claims to originality and influence? An alternative canon[1] of accelerated achievement that we could have arrived at sooner, with the help of a greater breadth of reference points? It's essential, of course, that we challenge received notions by amplifying underrepresented voices. One might use that argument to make the case for repositioning *Grimes* as an important English reference point in accounts of twentieth-century crossover opera traditionally dominated by the New York avant-garde, or Britten as a pioneer of queer performance, or Slater as a more significant writer in post-war theatre history than posterity has permitted him to be. But Britten is such an establishment and politically problematic figure that this doesn't feel like a story which urgently needs to be told – in the manner of the relatively recent recovery of the game-changing women writers of the Restoration and Romantic eras, say, or the African-American origins of popular music.

A better reason for starting the end of this book with David Lynch is that this highlights the slippery ways I have drawn upon different art forms throughout. The basis of my argument for the insertion of an opera into the theatre canon has been its influence on literature, art and now television too. These stepping stones suggest that there might be a wider truism about form to be uncovered, here, if we can pull back from the specificities of opera and theatre. If we can relax our focus until the point becomes purely that *Peter Grimes* inhabits two cultural traditions simultaneously, bridging them, blurring them, while drawing effects and energy from both, then Britten starts to look less like an obsessive master crafts-man, and more like a curious, playful polymath.

Of course, he's always looked a bit like that: contributor to film and theatre in the first decade of his career; artistic director, librettist and pedagogue later on. But what hasn't been widely acknowledged is that this version of Britten created mature masterpieces like *Peter Grimes* too: work that has tradition-ally been regarded as pure, undistracted composition; as what happened when Britten finally arrived at a place – Suffolk! – where he was allowed to focus fully on a single form. What if an important portion of the genius of at least one of these works, though, is precisely the product of its straddling relationship with two artistic shapes? Just as *Grimes* also twists unforgettable music out of the tensions between dappled English pastoralism and hard-edged European modernism, transgressive storytell-ing and a repressed, buttoned-up vernacular.

The spring of 2017 saw an exhibition at Two Temple Place in London with the title 'Sussex Modernism'. It attempted to trace, between the artists who made that county their home in the first half of the twentieth century, the same kind of lines as those which I used to sketch the Suffolk renaissance that sprang up in the second. Propped up in the middle of the first room, the starting point of the exhibition's argument, was a pair of stone garden rollers carved by Eric Gill. One review called them 'extraordinarily silly' (*Time Out*) and it was dif-ficult to disagree: could there be a more eloquent illustration of the whimsical priorities and tweedy paradoxes of English modernism than its most deviant figure's decision to express himself not only in sculpture and woodcuts but also with a couple of big old tools for turf? But I think they make a point, too, about interesting and powerful energies of English art in the twentieth century, as well as its shortcomings.

Perhaps it's because of the incalculable influence of the Arts and Crafts movement, so uninhibited in its application of intellectual principles to as many creative pursuits as possible. No doubt it's also partly thanks to the (not entirely unrelated) stomping spirit of generalist Victorian amateurism, which was still prevalent in the first decades of the twentieth century. But it's unarguable that many of the major figures of various English avant-gardes became enthusiastic polymaths and multi-form dabblers, leaping out of their areas of expertise into architecture and design, economics and psychoanalysis, gardening and fashion, photography and publishing, curation and cinema, science and spiritualism.[2] Which isn't to say that this was an energy that existed only in Britain: the most important twentieth-century reconfiguration of Arts and Crafts principles was, after all, the Bauhaus in Germany. But the tendency was sufficiently entrenched in English culture that it endured well into the post-war decades, where it might be spotted in Mervyn Peake's journey from illustration to writing, say, or Victor Pasmore's increasingly architectural ambitions, or John Betjeman flitting between poetry, heritage and broadcasting, or the jazz singer George Melly moonlighting as an art critic. Or indeed in John Piper's pivot from painting and stained glass to set design, for Britten.

In October 1934, the composer had visited the great European capitals of culture for the first time, and discovered that most of his long-held suspicions about English complacency and amateurism were well-founded. 'I felt so sorry for you', he wrote to a friend back home, 'with those London orchestras!' (cited in Kildea, 97). His unwillingness to indulge the cultural establishment of his homeland meant his relationship with many of its institutions and audiences remained prickly for much of his lifetime. English art was willing to accommodate him properly only once he'd died, and could be safely historicised. But that didn't mean he eschewed its games completely; that he didn't tap into the enthusiastically scatterbrained national attitude to form when he could see that a project would need to draw on more than just the usual if it was to, say, alter the course of modern opera. Perhaps the most significant new truth to take from the revelation that *Peter Grimes* represents a triumph in two forms, a great work of theatre as well as opera, is the suggestion that Britten was a truly English artist.

Notes

1 In our case, it might imagine an earlier manifestation of Peter Shaffer's *Amadeus*'s exploration of character through music, music through character; or Jez Butterworth's *Jerusalem*'s articulation of an Englishness rooted in the patterns and energies of landscape and history and besieged by the social, economic and political pressures of modern, bourgeois life.

2 A recent article about the Souls, a typical turn-of-the-century coterie of aristocrats and intellectuals, contains an evocative illustration of this phenomenon: 'They made a continuous show of effortless ability that is oddly suggestive of laziness: Cynthia Asquith remembered as a child waking early one morning and opening a window to see her uncle George Wyndham running circuits in the garden below: "Come out and join me", he shouted, "and then help me write an Aubade before breakfast"' (*London Review of Books*, 31 March 2016).

Bibliography

Books

Banks, Paul (editor): *The Making of Peter Grimes: Essays and Studies* (Woodbridge: The Boydell Press, 1996)

Billington, Michael: *State of the Nation: British Theatre Since 1945* (London: Faber, 2007)

Blythe, Ronald: *Akenfield: Portrait of an English Village* (London: Penguin, 2005)

Blythe, Ronald: *The Time by the Sea: Aldeburgh 1955–1958* (London: Faber, 2014)

Britten, Benjamin: *Peter Grimes/Gloriana: English National Opera Guide 24* (London: Overture Publishing, 2011)

Crabbe, George, Reginald Heber and Robert Pollok: *The Poetical Works of Crabbe, Heber, and Pollok, Complete in One Volume* (Philadelphia: Grigg and Elliot, 1839)

Crossley-Holland, Kevin (introduction to): *Peter Grimes: The Poor of the Borough* (London: Folio, 1990)

Fitzgerald, Penelope: *The Bookshop* (London: Fourth Estate, 2014)

Goorney, Howard: *The Theatre Workshop Story* (London: Eyre Methuen, 1981)

Graham, Scott and Steven Hoggett: *The Frantic Assembly Book of Devising Theatre* (London: Routledge, 2009)

Kerman, Joseph: *Opera as Drama* (Berkeley: University of California Press, 1988)

Kildea, Paul: *Benjamin Britten: A Life in the Twentieth Century* (London: Penguin, 2014)

Lee, Hermione: *Penelope Fitzgerald: A Life* (London: Random House, 2013)

Marland, Michael: *Peter Grimes: A Dramatization of the Poems by George Crabbe in* The Borough (London: Heinemann Educational, 1971)

Redner, Gregg Pierce: *Deleuze and Film Music: Building a Methodological Bridge between Film Theory and Music* (University of Exeter PhD, 2008)

Sebald, W. G.: *The Rings of Saturn* (London: The Harvill Press, 1998)

Slater, Montagu: *Peter Grimes, and Other Poems* (London: John Lane, 1946)

van Elferen, Isabella: *Popular Ghosts: The Haunted Spaces of Everyday Culture* (New York: Continuum, 2010)

Wagner, Richard: *Opera and Drama* (London: Dodo Press, 2008)

Wilson, Edmund: *Europe Without Baedeker: Sketches Among the Ruins of Italy, Greece and England, With Notes from a Diary of 1963–4: Paris. Rome. Budapest* (New York: Farrar, Straus and Giroux, 1966)

Zarrilli, Phillip B., Bruce McConachie, Gary Jay Williams and Carol Fisher Sorgenfrei: *Theatre Histories: An Introduction*, second edition (London: Routledge, 2006)

Articles

Ashley, Tim: 'Britten The Rape of Lucretia' (*Gramophone*)

Battle, Laura: 'Pierre-Laurent Aimard on Aldeburgh and Britten' (*Financial Times*, 23 May 2014)

Clements, Andrew: 'Grimes on the Beach – review' (*Guardian*, 18 June 2013)

Crewe, Tom: 'Aubade before Breakfast' (*London Review of Books*, 31 March 2016)

Gardner, Lyn: 'An Inspector Calls review – Stephen Daldry helps make the case for justice' (*Guardian*, 13 November 2016)

Handel, Darrell: 'Britten's use of the Passacaglia' (*Tempo*, October 1970)

Hochstrasser, Tim: 'Review: The Cocktail Party, Print Room at the Coronet' (*British Theatre*, 23 September 2015)

Loomis, George: 'Staging of Peter Grimes on the Beach Pays Tribute to Britten at 100' (*New York Times*, 25 June 2013)

Lynskey, Dorian: '"Make it like the wind, Angelo": How the Twin Peaks soundtrack came to haunt music for nearly 30 years' (*Guardian*, 24 March 2017)

Macfarlane, Robert: 'Robert Macfarlane's Untrue Island: the voices of Orford Ness' (*Guardian*, 8 July 2012)

Platt, Russell: 'Benjamin Britten's Moonrise Kingdom' (*The New Yorker*, 6 August 2012)

Rosenthal, Tom: 'Who was the real Peter Grimes?' (*Independent*, 26 June 2004)

Waywell, Chris: 'Sussex Modernism: Retreat and Rebellion' (*Time Out*)

Productions

Amadeus, directed by Michael Longhurst (National Theatre, 2016)

An Inspector Calls, directed by Stephen Daldry (National Theatre, 2015 revival of 1992 production)

Four Sea Interludes, video by Tal Rosner (Aldeburgh Festival, 2015)

Grimes on the Beach, directed by Tim Albery (Aldeburgh Festival, 2013)

Jerusalem, directed by Ian Rickson (Royal Court, 2009)

Peter Grimes, directed by David Alden (English National Opera, 2014 revival of 2009 production)

Satyagraha, directed by Phelim McDermott (English National Opera, 2013 revival of 2007 production)

The Borough, directed by Felix Barrett and Katy Balfour (Punchdrunk/ Aldeburgh Festival, 2013)

The Cocktail Party, directed by Abbey Wright (Print Room, 2015)

The Deep Blue Sea, directed by Carrie Cracknell (National Theatre, 2016)

The Magic Flute, directed by Simon McBurney (English National Opera, 2016 revival of 2013 production)

The Rape of Lucretia, directed by Fiona Shaw (Glyndebourne Festival, 2015 revival of 2013 production)

Uncle Vanya, directed by Rimas Tuminas (Vakhtangov State Academic Theatre of Russia, 2012)

Films

Akenfield, directed by Peter Hall (Angle Films Limited, 1974)

Love from a Stranger, directed by Rowland V. Lee (Trafalgar Film Productions Limited, 1937)

Moonrise Kingdom, directed by Wes Anderson (Indian Paintbrush, 2012)

Patience (After Sebald), directed by Grant Gee (Illuminations Films, 2012)

Perfect Lives, directed by Robert Ashley (Robert Ashley, Carlota Schoolman and The Kitchen, 1984)

Twin Peaks, directed by David Lynch (Lynch/Frost Productions, 1990)

Index